MAYA for Travelers and Students

Maya

FOR TRAVELERS
AND STUDENTS

A Guide to Language
and Culture in Yucatan

By Gary Bevington

The University of Texas Press, Austin

Requests for permission to reproduce material from this work
should be sent to Permissions, University of Texas Press,
Box 7819, Austin, TX 78713-7819.

⊗ The paper used in this publication meets the minimum
requirements of American National Standard for Information
Sciences—Permanence of Paper for Printed Library Materials,
ANSI Z39.48-1984.

Library of Congress Cataloging-in-Publication Data

Bevington, Gary Loyd.
    Maya for travelers and students : a guide to language and
culture in Yucatan / Gary Bevington. — 1st ed.
        p.   cm.
    Includes bibliographical references and index.
    ISBN 0-292-70838-6 (alk. paper). — ISBN 0-292-70812-2 (pbk. :
alk. paper)
    1. Maya language—Conversation and phrase books—English.
2. Mayas—Social life and customs.   3. Yucatán Peninsula—
Description and travel.   4. Yucatán Peninsula—Social life and
customs.   I. Title.
PM3965.B48   1995
497'.415—dc20   93-48159

Contents

Preface

This guide is for doing something, namely getting to know the Maya of the Yucatan peninsula through their language. I am still in the process of doing this myself and have written the book to a large extent as a way of working through and systematizing my own experience. My main principle in designing the organization and content of this guide is what kind of information I have found useful or would have found useful, had it been available. Because the basis is experiential, the book is undoubtedly biased and may misrepresent some things because it generalizes what I have encountered. While I have traveled extensively on the peninsula, my experience of daily life has been in one community and its environs. I am sure that if I had worked out of a community in the state of Campeche or in the Puuc region of Yucatan, some things in the book would be different.

A few remarks are needed about the Spanish in the book. This is not a book about the Spanish language per se, but it has a fair amount of Spanish in it. Since, unlike Maya, Spanish is a standardized language, I have to the extent possible tried to use a colloquial form of Mexican Spanish that would be intelligible to most Maya bilinguals without using non-standard Spanish forms that they might use themselves. For example, for the subjunctive of *haber,* the Maya themselves use *haiga* while I have used the standard *haya.* There are rare cases where I have found that even Maya who speak fluent, colloquial Spanish do not know the Spanish term for something that they know in Maya. An example is *t'oon* 'calf (of the leg)'. For this I simply gave the standard Spanish dictionary gloss *pantorilla.* In other cases, I have given both the local Spanish term and the dictionary term, e.g., *us* 'gnat' is locally *za(n)cudito* but *jején* in standard Spanish. In general, when I use 'Spanish' I mean Mexican Spanish synchronically. Many of the terms like *te-*

pezcuintle are etymologically Nahuatisms or other nativisms that have so enriched the Spanish of Mexico. My Spanish is not good, and my sense of level and style is even worse because I do not really use Spanish except as a means for my research in Yucatan. But I have made some decisions on my own about how to represent the Spanish, again based on my own experience. I beg the indulgence of readers whose sense of Spanish style may be offended by the Spanish in the book.

In glossing usage examples in both English and Spanish, I have used a more colloquial language than in the lexical glosses, trying to render, in English and Spanish, the way people generally say something in Maya. Thus, *paal* in the usage examples is often 'kid' or 'chico' instead of 'child' or 'niño'. Again I beg the reader's indulgence. Also, the glosses for Maya words may vary throughout the book because of the context in which they are used and because the material in the glossary is highly compressed and simplified, as in most introductory language presentations.

The existence of this book owes much to my wife Emöke. It was she who got me to go, very reluctantly, to Yucatan nine years ago for a week of spring vacation with our children. All of us eventually discovered our interests there, and our enthusiasm for the peninsula may have been the single major commonality of our fragmented "molecular" family through three trying adolescences. Em acted as interpreter when I knew little or no Spanish during my early work and later as the biggest critic of my presentation and strongest supporter of the project embodied in this book. Much of the material has been shamelessly taken from what she has related to me from her own experience. Jeffrey Himmelstein, a herpetologist and fellow denizen of the Quintana Roo forest known to the Maya as *Chuk Kan* ("Catches Snakes"), was very helpful with the literature on the flora and fauna of the peninsula.

Several experts have read and criticized drafts of the book, including an anonymous reader for the University of Texas Press, Brian Strosz, Paul Sullivan, and Carl Franz. Their criticisms have been most helpful and have certainly substantially improved the quality of the guide, but the errors of fact and misjudgments of interpretation are mine alone.

The greatest debt of gratitude I have is, however, to the people of Cobá, Quintana Roo, and its environs, who at first patiently tolerated and eventually warmly supported the peculiar notion of a gringo who kept returning twice a year to hang around and try to learn their language. Hopefully, many of my readers will repay their efforts by visiting that particular Maya community—which has so gracefully balanced accepting a steady stream of visitors with maintaining its cultural and linguistic integrity—along with the many other Maya communities on the peninsula.

MAYA for Travelers and Students

Introduction

The ascendancy of tourism on the Yucatan peninsula of Mexico in the past fifteen years has been nothing short of phenomenal, and with good reason, because it is simply a place which offers almost unlimited opportunity for an almost unbelievably wide range of tourist activities. With the spread of high-glitz, flash-and-trash tourism of the type associated on the peninsula with Cancun, some people have begun to worry about what the consequences of such tourism are both for the persons and places hosting the tourism as well as for the tourists themselves. The outgrowth of these concerns in the past couple of years has been a movement toward encouraging a kind of tourism that respects the natural and social environment of the places being visited and gives tourists the opportunity to develop a deeper understanding of and respect for the places which they visit. The movement toward such tourism has come to be known informally as "eco-tourism," and it is in the spirit of eco-tourism that the present guide to the Maya language and its speakers is offered to you.

The idea for it grew out of conversations with my friend Carl Franz, author of *The People's Guide to Mexico* and other works supporting low-budget, close-to-the-people tourism in Mexico. Carl and his partner, Lorena Havens, had been touring Yucatan with small groups and by themselves for some time. Despite a lot of contact with Maya speakers and a real desire to learn some of the language, they hadn't really made much progress. I asked Carl what materials he had been using, and he told me none because the only thing he knew of in print was Alfred Tozzer's *Maya Grammar* and he couldn't make any sense out of it. This I could certainly understand, and so I offered him a copy of what I considered the most accessible sketch of the language, a chapter from an unpublished grammar by Manuel Andrade. Carl took it with some hopes but reported to me that he couldn't make sense out of that either. Carl is a very intelligent person with a lot of experience in Mexico and particularly in Yucatan. He has learned to speak very good Spanish from limited adult-education classwork and a lot of practice in Mexico and Guatemala. He is a concerned and enthusiastic leader of the eco-tourist movement and was, in fact, an eco-tourist long before there was a name for it. I decided, therefore, to use Carl as my standard for intelligibility, and I have profited from his responses to the various parts of this guide as I was writing it.

Let me outline here the assumptions that I make in this guide about you, the user. First, I assume that you can read and understand the English text, which I have attempted to write at a level which would be appropriate for college undergraduates. Second, I expect that you will remember basic terms from school grammar, such as "noun," "verb," "clause," and so forth. I introduce some necessary technical terms to describe the language, but I give a brief definition or explanation at the outset. Finally, I expect you to know *some* Spanish. It doesn't have to be good Spanish (in fact, if you are fluent in Castillian or educated Mexican Spanish, this may turn out to be a disadvantage; see Chapter 2), but it has to be basic, usable, get-along-in-Mexico-type Spanish. If you don't know any Spanish for traveling, then you don't have any business starting Maya yet. Put this book away and take a Spanish course or get a travelers' guide to Spanish and travel with it until you feel that you can get along o.k. in that language. You need to have some Spanish to learn Maya for several reasons that will become apparent as we continue here.

The term "Maya" (or "Mayan"—that's just an adjective form) has been used for a long time in two distinct but interrelated ways that can be confusing. One way the term is used is to refer to a family of genetically related but distinct languages (theoretically, they came from a common ancestor language) and their speakers. The geographic area inhabited by speakers of these languages extends from northern Honduras in the south to the mountains of Guatemala and the state of Chiapas in southern Mexico in the west to the Yucatan peninsula in the north and east. There are also a couple of Maya languages spoken outside this geographic area (the technical term is "isolates") such as Huastec spoken north of

Veracruz. Exactly how many such languages there are and their relationship to one another are technical questions that we won't pursue here. In the highland part of the Maya area, i.e., Guatemala and Chiapas, the geographical area of the individual languages is often quite small, and so the speakers there have names for their particular language and its speakers, such as Tzotzil, Tzeltal, Quiché, Mam, etc. In Yucatan, the language of the indigenous population has a fairly wide geographic distribution, and the speakers of this language call it simply "Maya." Hence, the ambiguity arises between the family of languages called "Maya" and the language of the Yucatan peninsula also called "Maya." There are various devices that have been used by scholars to disambiguate the term. One such attempt, which failed, was to introduce the term "Mayance" for the family, keeping "Maya" for the language. The current accepted terminology is to call the language "Yucatec" or "Yucatec Maya," saving "Maya" for the family. The problem with this, though, is that it is confusing because, from the native perspective, the Spanish equivalent, *yucateco*, means a person from or living on the peninsula whether or not she or he is Maya. Since we are concerned here only with the language spoken on the peninsula, we will use the term "Maya" to mean the indigenous language spoken there and the culture group of its speakers. When you look at other sources, however, remember that "Maya" or "Mayan language" probably means the family or any member thereof, and the languages can be as different from "Yucatec Maya" as English is from Swedish.

Who Speaks Maya?

To start geographically, the indigenous (non-European or other immigrant) population in the modern Mexican states of Yucatan, Quintana Roo, and most of Campeche are Mayas. Obviously, to be racially a Maya is not to be equated with being a Maya, however. Those persons in this area (and the rest of Mexico, for that matter) who have culturally and linguistically moved away from the traditional life (see Chapter 1) are called *mestizos* (roughly, 'racially mixed'). Despite this term's obvious racial origin, the practical use of the designation today in Mexico means a person who no longer identifies himself or herself as *indígena* but rather as a cultural Mexican. There are therefore plenty of people who are almost pureblood Indians in Mexico who are not identified as such, and conversely there are people with a substantial amount of white blood who are Indians because of the way they live and the culture that they identify themselves with. Furthermore, on the peninsula *mestizo* has come to have another meaning; namely, it is used as a term for a social class, roughly 'working class', rather than as a racial or ethnic term.

At this point, a word of caution is in order about Spanish ethnic terminology. The Spanish equivalent of the English word 'Indian' is *indio*, but even more than the English word, it is now considered inappropriate. Calling someone an *indio* in Spanish may be taken to be a real insult. The official euphemism is *indígena*, an indigeneous person. There are, however, plenty of *indígenas* in Mexico who always use the word *indio* just as most Native Americans in the United States use the word 'Indian'. Although I use 'Indian' with my Native American friends and associates in the United States who use it themselves, the best advice is probably to avoid the use of *indio*, even if the *indígena* you're talking to uses it. There may be an element of self-deprecation in its use. With others in Mexico, always use *indígena* to avoid any hint of being taken for a bigot (on ethnic terminology in Maya, see Chapter 5, People). Anyway, the long and the short of it is that one who lives, acts, and speaks like a Maya is a Maya. In western Campeche, there are indigenous people who speak another Maya language, Chontal, and are therefore, by our working definition, not Maya.

Certain general principles tell whether a person is likely to speak Maya. First, with respect to lifestyle, a rural person who lives off the land by making a milpa (Spanish term borrowed into English, see Chapter 5, Work, for Maya equivalent) is the most likely to speak Maya as his dominant language. In fact, the Maya monolinguals (i.e., those who speak no Spanish) are almost exclusively from this class. Agricultural workers and day-laborers (and their families, obviously) are also fairly likely to know and use Maya. At the other end, business and professional people are the least likely to know and use Maya, except where geographic factors enter in. The colonial cities such as Mérida, Campeche, and Valladolid are the places where Maya is less in use than in other

places. In the modern tourist centers such as Cancun and Cozu-
mel, Maya is known only by people who would probably rather
forget that they do know it. In the rural areas as one moves east
and south from Mérida, the use of Maya increases. In the central
and particularly the inland part of Quintana Roo (the center of the
so-called Zona Maya is the city of Felipe Carrillo Puerto) Maya is
used almost exclusively, and here is where the largest population
of Maya speakers knowing little or no Spanish is to be found.

These are the general principles by which one can determine the likelihood of a person's speaking Maya. After a while one develops a pretty good intuitive sense of whether or not an individual uses Maya in daily life. You should also be aware that for a long time many white people in Yucatan also spoke Maya, making it one of the few places in the New World where an indigenous language became the medium of communication between native people and the conquerors. Today there are still people who don't look or live like traditional Maya yet who can speak the language. Often they learned Maya as kids playing with Maya children. Many such people as adults use Spanish, however, with the Maya who speak it, and so you can't even tell from the language of address. Typically, I learn that such people speak Maya because they hear me speaking with my Maya friends, and they want to try speaking Maya with me as a matter of curiosity.

In general, initiating speaking Maya with someone who might not speak Maya as a main medium of communication is to be avoided. Service personnel in Cancun, for example, should never be addressed in Maya without judicious inquiry in Spanish first. The best rule is save your Maya for when you're away from the flash and trash of the resorts and the hustle and bustle of the cities. Anyone who sees himself or herself as official or important or so-phisticated, such as a cop, civil administrator, or government em-ployee, should be addressed in Spanish everywhere. Don't force your Maya on anyone; if they want to speak Spanish or even try their English on you, go with the flow. This is not an issue for militance in Mexico, as language rights are in, say, parts of Europe or Asia. Everyone accepts the idea that Spanish is *the* language of Mexico and should be used unless the parties speaking agree on using some other language, just like English in the United States.

Finally, it should be added that Maya is also spoken outside of Mexico in Belize and in the Petén area of Guatemala. The party line among modern scholars is that the form of Maya spoken in El Petén is a distinct language which they call "Itza Maya." It doesn't make any difference to us, however, because there is but a handful of speakers left there. The same is largely true in Belize, although in northern Belize around Corozal Town there are descen-dants of Maya refugees from the Caste War (see below) who still know Maya.

Historical Background

Maya has been spoken on the Yucatan peninsula for a very long time, certainly for a long time before the Spanish arrived in the sixteenth century. A high civilization developed in this area in the early part of our era (from the third century on) which counted among its achievements the development of a writing system, which we now call "Hieroglyphic Maya." An important question is what was the spoken language on which Hieroglyphic Maya was based. For a long time, scholars agreed that Hieroglyphic Maya was a purely logographic system; i.e., each symbol represented a word. This meant that the question of the language was relatively unimportant for the real problem of deciphering the glyphs, and it became the custom to name the glyphs using a Yucatec Maya word that corresponded meaningwise to the interpretation of the glyph. The view that the hieroglyphs were strictly logographic, however, turned out to be incorrect. In the past fifteen years a major breakthrough in the interpretation of Hieroglyphic Maya was achieved with the recognition of numerous phonetic elements in the system. This means that the question of the spoken language is indeed crucial to interpretation. There has been a shift away from seeing Hieroglyphic Maya as simply the immediate predecessor of our Maya, but a real consensus on what the language base of the hieroglyphs was has yet to emerge. Whatever it was, however, it was close to the Maya of Yucatan, and so with a bit of generalization that ignores some details, we can say that Maya has a longer written history than either English or Spanish.

At the time of the conquest, the use and knowledge of the hieroglyphs were apparently in decline, and so when the padres taught some of the Maya to read and write using Latin letters, this writing system was converted by them for their own use as well. A fairly extensive collection of written documents in Maya from the sixteenth through nineteenth century survives, and the language represented in these colonial documents is sometimes called "Classical" or "Colonial Maya." The most interesting documents from this period are the books of Chilam Balam. There are a number of these books which were discovered in the nineteenth and twentieth centuries and are preserved either in the original or in copies. The Chilam Balam books were kept secretly by the

Maya in various settlements of colonial Yucatan and recopied as the earlier copies disintegrated in the climate. The copies were imperfect and new material from the colonial Christian tradition was introduced, but the books are clearly the maintenance of a precolonial indigenous tradition of record-keeping. The language of the Chilam Balam books is very obscure, and speakers of the modern language find them unintelligible without the kind of help that English speakers need reading Old or Middle English. The works are usually referred to by the town the manuscript was found in, e.g. "The Chilam Balam of Chumayel."

After the collapse of the Spanish colonial empire in the early nineteenth century, Yucatan vacillated between being an independent state and a part of Mexico. The shift in the economic base of the area after the collapse led to intensified oppression of the Maya by the white population. As a result, a race war known as the Caste War (La guerra de castas) engulfed the peninsula in the second half of the 1840s. During the time of Mexico's war with the United States, the white population was nearly driven from the peninsula by the Maya, but then the tide shifted in favor of the whites. Beginning in about 1850 those Maya who were still in rebellion against the whites formed independent states of their own design in the eastern part of the peninsula. The most important of the states was centered around a town which the rebels built called Chan Santa Cruz. The Cruzob (as the rebels called themselves) established a theocratic state based on their cult of talking crosses.

Remarkably, the Chan Santa Cruz state existed for half a century until a Mexican expeditionary force was sent in to crush the rebels. Rather than face certain annihilation in the face of the overwhelming firepower of the Mexican army, the rebels simply abandoned the town of Chan Santa Cruz and melted into the surrounding forest. The official date for the pacification of the rebelling Indians is 1937, when the most beloved of modern Mexican presidents, Lázaro Cárdenas, made peace with the Indians. In fact, the military theocracy of the Cruzob is still maintained in a few villages around the town of Felipe Carrillo Puerto, which is the modern name of Chan Santa Cruz. The importance of these historical events for the language is that some Maya lived completely outside Mexican authority until comparatively recently. This has given the language a political base which is unique among the indigenous languages of the New World, for the Caste War and the subsequent establishment of the Indian states must be considered the only successful Indian rebellion against the Europeans in history.

1. Learning Indigenous Languages

Since I assume that you have followed my advice to learn some Spanish before undertaking the task of learning some Maya, you already have some experience with learning a foreign language. But your foreign language experience is probably with major European languages (Spanish, French, German, etc.) and probably in a formal instructional setting (high school, college, adult education, etc.). Therefore I want to offer some discussion here of differences between learning an indigenous language on your own and the more usual situation.

Although there is a long written tradition for Maya, it is probably more realistic to think of the modern language as essentially unwritten. Of course, this is not strictly true; people do write Maya, and there is even an academy concerned with the preservation and standardization of the language to some extent. But the use of written Maya is really almost negligible, restricted to a few Maya intellectuals who are concerned with these activities. In the rural areas there are schools that purport to be "*escuelas bilingües*," but teaching literacy skills in Maya is not taken very seriously by the instructional staff, which is for the most part young Mexicans doing their national service.

The effect of having a literate linguistic culture is that it tends to establish a certain form or range of forms as the standard, or "good," form of the language, all other forms then being diminished in prestige as "dialects," or non-standard versions of the language. It behooves foreigners learning a language to orient their efforts toward a recognized standard form of the language. With indigenous languages such standard forms do not exist or, if they do, are so unknown that you probably would not be understood using them. You therefore must pay attention to observing and imitating native practice in language use and to using the language to make yourself understood (also see Chapter 2).

Psychologically, learning a language by using it is a major adjustment for adults. Most of us are accustomed to controlling our world verbally, and after a lifetime of practice we get very good at it. We know how to flatter, threaten, request, demand, insult, praise, inform, deceive, wheedle, cajole, etc., according to our best assessment of what is necessary to get the job done. To begin to use another language to do this means in some ways that you are abandoning a lifetime of knowledge and experience with your native language to confront the world with an extremely limited set of linguistic tools. The insecurity is compounded by the fact that the world which one is confronting is also not completely familiar. You know from learning and using Spanish, for example, that getting things done in Mexico and elsewhere in the Spanish-speaking world is different from getting them done at home.

In the case of learning indigenous languages like Maya you have the additional complication of a qualitatively different situation known as a "small-scale culture." For us in the United States, the differences between what goes on in California, North Dakota, and Alabama are not really that major. Mass media, education, and travel give us access to innovations not just in our own country but, to some extent, in the entire world, because our broad Anglo-American macro-culture has, in some sense, become the medium of exchange for a large part of the world. For the traditional Maya, life is hard but simple and orderly, and they feel very comfortable with their way of living as long as it provides enough to sustain them. Change and innovation are not sought out, although when opportunities such as electrification are provided, the Maya are happy to discover the benefits. But what is happening in Mérida or Mexico City, to say nothing of Washington or London, is really very remote, if not unknown. This is not to say that they don't have a world in which they hope and dream and plan and worry, but their hopes and dreams and plans and concerns are other than ours.

The result is that you are coming to the task of experiencing a bit of the Maya world using the Maya language, and the tools that served you so well at home are largely inoperative. You have to be prepared to make mistakes, make a fool of yourself, be not understood or misunderstood, and lack the basic kind of control of situations which you have at home. You have to listen and watch, try to understand the bases of behaviors, and learn to respond appropriately. If you do, of course, this kind of learning can be a very rewarding experience, not just in terms of understanding more about the world around you, but ultimately in terms of understanding yourself.

Here are some practical suggestions for successful encounters with indigenous peoples:

1. Read to become as informed as you can before and during your experience. Remember, however, that just because some "expert" (including me) says things work in a particular way does not make it true. The line between a social-science generalization and a stereotype is an elusive one at best. A characterization, even a well-intentioned one by an expert with profound experience and knowledge, will not be true everywhere all the time.

2. Learn to keep your mouth shut and your eyes and ears open. Periods of silence do not necessarily make traditional people as uncomfortable as they might people in our culture.

3. Develop a system to work through what you experience. One way to do this is in written form: note keeping or journal writing. Another is to discuss it with other gringos doing the same or similar things. It is not a bad idea to carry three-by-five-inch file cards or a small notebook and *unobtrusively* jot down information about things as soon as possible after you experience them.

4. Remember that from the native perspective you are an odd thing that dropped from the sky into the middle of their well-ordered and busy world. You are disruptive and confusing because people of your ilk are expected to be remote and generally disdainful of their world. The fact is that a few brief visits over a long period of time will make you become a real and maybe even eventually welcome visitor. Our tendency is to want to go at things in a concentrated, expeditious manner, and this is, in this case, exactly the wrong way of doing things.

5. Say what you mean and don't make extravagant gestures. Unlike the Mexican or American custom of saying you intend to do something in the future that you probably won't be able or want to do, traditional people like the Maya admire modesty and consequence. Try to respect that. Be as punctual in appointments as circumstances allow. On the other hand, you must be prepared to deal gracefully with being "stood up" for a meeting or an appoint-

ment. One way to tell how serious the Maya are about some future activity is the degree of precision with which they want to pin down the time and place for it. Rather than saying no to a proposal, they will simply be vague about its realization. Take this as a sign to wind down your side of the negotiations on it.

6. Other than shaking hands, do not initiate physical contact. If someone puts his or her hand on your back or embraces you, respond accordingly. Be especially circumspect with adults of the opposite sex.

7. Be sensitive to the gender roles that the culture recognizes. Among the Maya, as in most traditional cultures, men and women relate to one another in clearly defined but limited ways. The role of dealing with the outside world is primarily a man's role, and since whether male or female you are part of the outside world, most of the Maya with whom you will be able to make contact will be men. The anomaly that Western or Westernized women present to traditional societies is typically resolved by simply treating them as "honorary" men. After all, they wear pants, sit with men, drink alcohol, drive cars, have jobs and careers, and do many other things that, except for biology, make them men from the traditional point of view.

If you are a woman, and if you want to get to know the traditional women's culture, look for an opportunity to develop a relationship with a mature traditional woman. This will probably require some deftness and perseverance on your part. One way might be to ask if you can sit with a group of women making tortillas at a fiesta (see Chapter 5, Celebrations). After a while you might ask if they would teach you how to make tortillas. They will be *very* curious about you, but they will act on their curiosity only to the extent that they feel comfortable with you. They are strongly oriented toward appearance, and the unusual features (from their perspective) of your physical being will be the object of their attention. Be prepared to deal with intense interest in your shaved legs (if you do shave), your jewelry, and so forth. One woman said to another about my wife: *Sak u yiich'ak*! 'Her fingernails are white!' Like all relationships, female friendships with traditional women take time and patience, but you can be rewarded with views of the distinctive support networks of traditional women.

8. Act in an open and consistent manner. While people in a remote village may know nothing of what is going on in the capi-

tal or abroad, everybody knows *everything* that goes on in their small-scale world. Since you are by your very nature an object of curiosity and wonder, people whom you have never met or maybe even seen may in fact know a surprising amount about you and your activities. Be aware that there are inevitably factions and tensions in small communities. It is important not to be drawn into such things. A village may, for example, be divided religiously into traditionalists/Catholics, on the one hand, and evangelical Protestants, on the other. It may be that you wish to spend more time with one group or the other. That is perfectly o.k., but also make an effort to have a cordial relationship with the other side. Above all, avoid anything that could be interpreted as proselytizing, whether religious or social. Remember that traditional Maya engage in binge drinking, they want only minimal formal education for their children, and men and women have well-defined gender roles that are not violated. If you see such things as "evils" in need of your attention, then I would urge you to restrict your activities to looking at the pyramids, snorkeling, and shopping for gifts, rather than seeking to get to know the people. If there are Mexican or American missionaries in the area, keep your distance without being hostile. Similar guidelines apply to the Mexican political parties.

2. Maya and Spanish

The influence of Spanish on the Maya language is strongest in the area of vocabulary. The range of the Spanish element in the Maya vocabulary is quite wide. Some words that any Maya speaker would assume to be "real" Maya are, in fact, of Spanish origin. A relatively straightforward example of this is the word 'cattle' (Spanish *ganado*): the Maya *wakax* must be a very early (sixteenth century?) adaptation of Spanish *vacas* 'cows' because, of course, the only domestic animals in the New World before the Contact were dogs and (maybe) turkeys. From the point of view of learning the language this fact is merely a historical curiosity of no significance to the task at hand.

The status of generally recognizable Spanish words in Maya can be characterized according to two general categories: form and function. From the point of view of form we distinguish between Mayanized Spanish loanwords and Spanish foreign words used in Maya. The loanwords have undergone pronunciation and/or formal (grammatical) changes that make them distinct from Spanish. An example of a pronunciation change would be the word *piitoo* 'whistle, flute' with elongated vowels and rising pitch on the final syllable, from Spanish *pito*. Formal changes can be seen in the Maya verb *maldisyontik* '(to) curse', which is from the Spanish noun *(la)maldición* '(the) curse' by adding the stem-forming suffix *-t* and the transitive incomplete suffix *-ik* as well as pronunciation changes. Functionally, there are Spanish words for which native equivalents do not exist and those for which they do. An example of a word for which there is no generally known and used native equivalent is *amigoo* 'friend'. The two categories are independent of each other (i.e., they don't correlate), and there is some gradation within each category, but we will not pursue the matter here any further. In addition to using Spanish words in Maya, there is also the practice of casually slipping back and forth between the two languages for larger linguistic chunks such as phrases, sentences, and whole groups of sentences. The technical name for intercalating two languages is "code-switching." This kind of Maya, larded with Spanish, is called *mestizo maya* 'mixed Maya' locally, as opposed to *maya puro* 'pure Maya'. In theory, one could lard Spanish with Maya and make something like Mayanized Spanish, but in fact this is not really done. If speech has any substantial amount of Maya in it, then it counts as Maya. Of course, there are characteristic non-standard forms of Spanish spoken by Maya-dominant people, but that is not our concern.

The question now is what the practical consequences of this code-switching are for learning to speak Maya. Let me deal with this by making a number of points:

1. You cannot speak intelligible Maya and talk about any real range of topics, even about the Maya world, without using Spanish words. *Maya puro* is a fiction, although there is obviously an enormous range in the amount of Spanish words and the kind of code-switching that various speakers use.

2. The best practice is to follow native speakers' practice to the extent possible. You should also feel free to switch to Spanish if you need to say something that you can't say in Maya, but ask yourself if you really need to say it at all, because excessive code-switching simply invites people to switch entirely to Spanish to help the gringo out.

3. One of the real benefits of your showing an interest in the Maya language is that it reinforces native linguistic awareness and pride. Many Maya parents make the tragic mistake of speaking only Spanish to their children and permitting the children to speak only Spanish for the reasonable but quite wrong idea that this increases the children's chances of success in school and later life. In fact, studies show that children who are raised bilingually have substantial cognitive advantages over monolingual children. This is not something to proselytize for, but I have seen gringo interest in Maya lead to substantial changes in attitude toward use of the language by children. If people obviously don't want to have Maya spoken to the children, then you should respect their wishes and speak Spanish to the children.

4. Strengthened pride in the language may also result in more awareness of gratuitous Spanish in the speech of individuals, par-

ticularly as you imitate their practice, because what they say then has consequences in terms of the way you speak the language. Let me give an example here. A friend wanted to let me know that he couldn't help me at the time because a coworker was taking a rest, and he said *Fredi tun deskansar.* 'Freddy is resting.' The use of the Spanish *descansar* is a typical example of daily gratuitous code-switching, and of course I acted as though nothing had happened. The next day I made a point of saying *Tin bin deskansar.* 'I am going to rest.', which brought the response *Tan a bin a he'saba.* 'You're going to rest.' in Maya.

5. However, you may run into some well-intentioned person who sees it as his duty to save you from mestizo Maya and teach you *"maya puro"* and coincidentally show you (and anyone else in earshot) his erudition. The problem with what you will learn from such a person is that its use will make you unintelligible to speakers of Maya, leaving aside the question of whether what he is teaching you has any historical or other reality. You can be sure that your would-be teacher does not speak that way himself for he would be held to ridicule by his peers. There are some relatively easy ways to find out if you are being led by the nose. If the person has Maya equivalents for such things as 'good morning', 'friend', and 'tape recorder' or can give you numbers above four, then you've got a pedant. The best thing to do is glaze over and politely move on.

6. In pronouncing Spanish words in Maya, there is a tendency to Mayanize the pronunciation by lengthening the vowels, substituting for certain Spanish consonants which Maya lacks and giving the word a "sing-song" pitch contour like in Maya. The degree to which any particular word receives such a Mayanized pronunciation depends upon several factors. First, the degree to which the word is perceived as integrated in Maya will determine whether it should be pronounced "Mayan." At the one extreme are technical terms used infrequently which are generally pronounced as they would be by the same person speaking Spanish. Typically such terms are used only by bilinguals anyway. At the other end are those items of Spanish vocabulary which are used daily and are really the only or the common term used in Maya. Our example of *amigoo* will do quite nicely here. In between there is a lot of variation. Speaking Spanish with a Maya accent is considered by non-Maya Mexicans as well as many would-be sophisticate bilin-

guals to be "rustic" and to identify the speaker as something of a rube. Exactly for this reason I have taken to Mayanizing Spanish words when they are amenable whether or not speakers use the words themselves. Let me give you my favorite example. I need to wear reading glasses to do close work. Glasses are almost never used among traditional Maya, although they certainly have seen them and know what they are. Not surprisingly, there is no Maya word for glasses, and the colloquial Spanish *gafas* must be used. I refer to my glasses as *in gaapaas* or even *in gaapaaso'ob* with a Mayan plural ending as well as a Spanish one. I can see that I am readily understood and that people find the usage pleasantly amusing. The hidden message is, of course, that I admire the native pronunciation by trying to imitate it rather than pronounce the Spanish word with a Mexican pronunciation.

You can sort out the details of Mayanizing the pronunciation of Spanish by listening, but I will give you a couple of examples to get you started. First, the labial fricatives *v* and *f*, which are not found in Maya, should be changed to the corresponding stops *b* and *p*. The substitution of *b* for *v* is very characteristic of Spanish spoken by the Maya. Keep this in mind when you speak Spanish with them, because their inability to make the *v* sound can be embarrassing to them if you act as though you have difficulty understanding them because of it. The same is not so true for *f*, but Maya-dominant speakers do occasionally replace it with *p* when speaking Spanish. Another characteristic of Maya pronunciation that gets carried over into Mayan Spanish is replacing word-final *n* with *m*, particularly if there is another labial sound nearby. Thus, *pan* 'bread' is often pronounced *pam*. The same principle applies to Maya words as well, and so *bin* 'go' is often pronounced *bim*. This last pronunciation characteristic appears to be something of a linguistic hallmark of particular social significance, much like "ain't" in English, and you may want to use it either in Maya or Spanish or avoid it according to the way you want to present yourself to people. Because the sound *r* is much less frequent in Maya than in Spanish, some Maya hyper-correct by using *r* in place of Spanish *l*, saying *swerdo* in Maya for Spanish *sueldo* 'salary'. Likewise, *alux* 'guardian of the milpa' (see Chapter 5, Work) may be pronounced *arux*.

7. You should be aware that sometimes differences can develop between a Maya word and its Spanish equivalent, especially so

when commercially produced objects are denoted. For example, the Maya word for pants is *eex* but for *some* Maya men's outerwear is *pantalon(es)*, and *eex* is then women's wear. Since Mayan women never wear slacks or shorts, it can only mean 'panties', for which the full term is *yeex ko'olel.* The alternative that this presents is to lard up one's Maya with a lot of Spanish nouns as many Maya do. Probably the best strategy is to try the Maya if you know it, and if you get a puzzled look from doing so, use the Spanish name for the thing.

3. Pronunciation and Spelling

Our primary interest in this guide is with the spoken rather than the written language. Although Maya has been written for a long time, even ignoring the hieroglyphic texts, there is really relatively little use made today of written Maya. For example, attempts at introducing Maya-language books, newspapers, and magazines have been very modest and generally unsuccessful. Except for some agricultural notices, there are almost no signs or public representations of the language. In the past twenty years or so the attempt has been made to introduce a "modern" alphabet for the indigenous languages of Mexico. It must be remembered that while (Yucatec) Maya and Nahuatl (the language of the Aztecs in the Valley of Mexico) have relatively rich colonial written traditions, most other Indian languages do not. The result of the reform is that a new alphabetic tradition for writing Maya now has the current stamp of approval, despite the fact that there is really very little written in it.

It should be pointed out that within each of the two traditions, Colonial and Modern, there is a fair amount of variation. Nevertheless, it is possible to specify each alphabetic tradition in terms of a few variant representations for a few sounds. The conventions used in writing any language are ultimately a relatively superficial matter as long as the system works for effective written communication among native speakers of the language. One need, I think, look no further than English to see that a system doesn't have to be completely rational nor does it have to represent all the facts of pronunciation to be effective. Nevertheless, the written form of the language may be a highly charged issue both politically and culturally. While the Maya and other indigenous people of Mexico are marginalized in terms of the greater society, they are generally not actively persecuted and oppressed, as their counterparts have been unfortunately in Guatemala. There the Mayan language academy representing all the Mayan language groups in the country has been a powerful symbol of native self-determination, and recently scholars in the United States and other developed countries have taken to using the orthographic conventions promulgated by the native language academies as a way of showing solidarity and support for self-determination even, for example, in writing about phonetic aspects of Hieroglyphic Maya. Despite the fact that I am uncomfortable with chucking the four-hundred-year tradition of the Colonial alphabet and replacing it with a "modern" alphabet that is written in virtually as fragmented variations as was the Colonial, in this book I used the version of the Modern alphabet that is found in the monumental Cordemex dictionary (see Further Reading). Keep in mind that all Mayan place names and personal names in Mexico continue to be publicly represented in the Colonial alphabet. For this reason, the place names on the map at the beginning of the book are given in their Colonial spellings. Also, all but a portion of the most recent literature on the pre-Columbian and Colonial Maya uses the Colonial alphabet in various versions. You will therefore find it to your advantage to become somewhat familiar with it also.

Vowels

In *quality* (the position of the lips, tongue, etc.) the vowels of Maya correspond almost perfectly to those of Spanish. The difference between them lies in the area of *quantity*, particularly in the length of the vowels. It must be emphasized that by length here, we really mean the relative duration of the sounds and *not* differences of tenseness and quality which are referred to as "long" and "short" vowels in English (e.g. 'bite' or 'beat' vs. 'bit'). Short vowels are represented with a single letter and long vowels with the letter doubled.

There are also long vowels which are pronounced, particularly in slow, careful pronunciation, with a "glottal stop" between the two vowels. A glottal stop is the sound made by blocking the breath stream off with the vocal bands, that is to say, the sound between the two vowels in 'uh-oh' (what English speakers say when they realize something is wrong) or the way many Americans pronounce the *t* in 'mountain' or 'button'. Finally, there are short vowels which end with a glottal stop. The difference between short and long vowels can be used to differentiate meaning in Maya. However, many vowels are lengthened on a somewhat *ad hoc* basis depending on their environment, the speech community, and the speaker. It is particularly characteristic to lengthen vowels in the speech in the eastern part of the peninsula, and this plays a role in the adaptation of Spanish words for use in Maya (see Chapter 2). Nevertheless, you should keep in mind that each vowel quality (*a, e, i, o, u*) has four realizations that have the potential to be distinctive in Maya: plain short, plain long, long interglottalized, and short postglottalized. I can't make this any easier because those are the facts, except to say that the practical potential for meaning confusion from the wrong vowel is relatively low. Try to imitate native speakers, but don't expect them to be consistent because in normal and rapid speech a lot of things get changed.

It may be instructive to contrast phonetically similar words in Spanish and Maya: for example, Spanish *malo* 'bad' vs. Maya *ma'aloob* 'it's o.k.'. Similar contrasts can be found in Maya between *kan* 'snake', *k'aan* 'hammock', *ka'an* 'sky', and *ha'* 'water'. Examples with other vowel qualities include: *ek'* 'star', *eek'* 'dirty', *kin we'esik* 'I show it', *tin he'skimba* 'I'm resting'; *kin bin* 'I go', *piim* 'thick', *xi'im* 'corn', *chi'* 'mouth'; *kol* 'milpa', *kook* 'deaf', *ko'ox* 'let's go', *tin ho'sik* 'I'm getting it out'; *kuch* 'load', *kuuk* 'elbow', *ku'uk* 'squirrel', *kin wu'yik* 'I hear it'.

Consonants

Many of the consonants also correspond quite closely to Spanish pronunciation, for example, the voiceless *p, t, ch,* and *k* in *polok* 'fat', *toot* 'mule', *chich* 'strong', and *kook* 'deaf'. The *k* is equivalent to the "hard" *c* of Spanish and is used in the Modern alphabet to avoid the confusion of the "soft" pronunciation before *i* and *e* or the use of *qu* as in Spanish. One additional sound in Maya is written *ts*, which is pronounced like the *ts* in English 'lets'. An example in a Maya word is *otsil* 'poor'.

The five Maya sounds presented so far—*p, t, ts, ch,* and *k*—also occur glottalized. Remember the glottal stop above ('uh-oh'). The glottal stop is articulated at the same time as each of the five sounds to give them a distinct "popping" quality, and these are then five quite distinct and different sounds in Maya that occur neither in Spanish nor in English. They are written respectively *p'*, *t'*, *ts'*, *ch'*, and *k'*. Maya words containing these sounds are *p'ok* 'hat', *t'uup* 'youngest brother, little finger', *ts'iib* 'writing', *ch'iich'* 'bird', *k'aak'* 'fire'. The difference is not always so clear, especially in normal speech (as opposed to slow, careful pronunciation), but for Maya speakers it is a *big* difference, so try to pay attention when you learn a word with glottalized sounds. In general over-doing the glottalization of the consonants is preferable to pro-nouncing them as they may sound to you when the Maya speak casually. The *b* is also glottalized, but the effect of glottalizing it is to make it sound a bit like it is being "swallowed" rather than "popped." Since unlike the other glottalized sounds there is no plain or unglottalized *b* for it to contrast with, it is not crucial that the glottalization be present when pronouncing the sound. Not glottalizing gives you a "foreign" accent in Maya, but you will have that in any case.

The *s* sound also occurs in Maya and is similar to the sound in Spanish (where it is also written *z* and *c*). There is also a sound like the initial sound in English 'shoe', and the letter *x* is used to represent it. The sound *l* is like Spanish except that it and the *b* tend to remain very weak or unpronounced at the end of words. The Maya *h* is like the English one, not the Spanish one (which is silent), although in Maya, unlike English, it occasionally occurs and is pronounced before consonants (e.g. *hmen* 'shaman', *nohchil* 'boss'). Maya uses the letter *w* for a sound that is quite like the English. The *y* is as in Spanish. The *r* is very rare in Maya (*urich* '[land] snail' is an unusual example) except in obvious Spanish bor-rowings where other sounds found in Spanish but foreign to Maya, such as *f*, *d*, and *g* ("hard" pronunciation), are not at all uncom-mon. The sound associated with Spanish *j* and *g* ("soft" pronun-ciation) also occurs marginally in Maya not only in Spanish bor-rowings but also in emphatic pronunciation of Maya *h* and in some onomatopoetic expressions. There is no conventional spell-ing for the sound, however.

The Modern Alphabet Variants

The *ts* and *ts'* are sometimes represented as *tz* and *tz'* respectively. The *h* is often represented *j*, apparently an attempt to make the system more Hispanic. Occasionally, the *x* is represented with the phonetic symbol *š* or even the English digraph *sh*.

The feature of pitch or tone (see Stress and Intonation, this chapter) does have the potential to make meaning-bearing distinctions. Because of this, some recent writings in Maya show the tones by the use of grave and acute accent marks over the vowels. Some writers show them on all vowels where it is appropriate, while others represent them only where there is the potential for ambiguity, much like the accent marks in the Spanish orthography. Because the potential for misunderstanding from misplaced tones is relatively low and they are really a feature best acquired by imitation of native speakers, who in any case show variation in their use, I have generally omitted the representation of prosody in this book.

The Colonial Alphabet and Variant Spellings

The hallmark of all forms of the Colonial alphabet is the use of *c* to represent the *k* sound. Note that the Colonial *c* is invariant, i.e. always "hard," so that the *c*'s in *ciic* 'sister' are the same as those in *cooc* (i.e. *kook* in the examples above) and not like *siis* 'cool'. Also, *tz* is always used for *ts*. The Colonial *k* then represents the corresponding glottalized sound, i.e., *k'* in the Modern alphabet. The other glottalized sounds, which do not correspond to anything in Spanish or other European languages, show most of the variation. Among the conventions tried were doubling letters (e.g. *pp*, *tt*, and *chh* [or *chch*] for *p'*, *t'*, and *ch'* respectively) or "barring" the letters (*p̵, ŧ, cħ*). The Modern *ts'* is represented either with *dz* or with the special letter ɔ in Colonial writing. Because of the phonetic equivalence of *s* and *z* in American Spanish as well as the soft pronunciation of the letter *c*, sometimes *z* or *ç* is used to represent the former sound. The *w* sound in Spanish does not have a distinct letter or letters to represent it, and so *w* is written *u* in the Colonial writing. Most of the time it is fairly easy to tell when the Colonial *u* is pronounced *w*, namely in the environment of vowels, while as a vowel in the environment of consonants. Occasional ambiguities did exist, however. For example, in the Colonial numbers (they are not used in Modern Maya, see Noun Phrase Modifiers, in the grammar) *uac* 'six' and *uuc* 'seven' are pronounced (Modern spelling) *wak* and *u'uk* (and not *wuk*) respectively. In the Colonial Maya writings the differences in vowel quantity and glottalization were largely ignored. When double vowels were written, they usually represented long interglottalized vowels.

This survey is summarized in tabular form below, using common phonetic terminology for those who have learned descriptive phonetics somewhere.

Finally, it is important to note that there is a substantial amount of variation in pronunciation even within a small Mayan speech community. Let me give you a few examples here. There is a strong tendency to drop certain consonants, namely *b* and *l*, when they end a word. Thus, the word *che'o'ob* 'trees' is usually pronounced *che'oo*, although the *b* is pronounced if a vowel is added after it, e.g., *le che'oobo'* 'the trees'. A somewhat different kind of variation is found with respect to the long interglottalized vowels in that the glottalization may be lost in any kind of speech except slow, careful pronunciation. Thus, some speakers will pronounce *mixba'al* as *mixbaal* in slow, careful pronunciation when you ask them to, but others reject this pronunciation, although in normal and rapid speech the word is typically pronounced as *mixbaa*. Also vowels, particularly plain short vowels, tend to be dropped in the middle of words as suffixes are added. The technical name for this is syncope, and it also happens in English, although the nuts and bolts of syncope in English and Maya are quite different. In English, when the "-ing" suffix is added to two-syllable words like 'sicken' and 'label', they are often pronounced "sickning" or "labling." There are, in fact, two versions of syncope in Maya: one obligatory even in careful speech, the other variable with the speed, care, and speech style of the speaker. The exact rules for syncope are too complicated to be worth your learning at this point. I have generally been quite conservative about showing syncope in the examples, but wherever it seems to you that a vowel is missing in the middle of a word, the absence is explainable as syncope. When you get to speaking Maya with the people, you will need to make additional adjustments for syncopated vowels, of course. A variation of syncope is the shortening of long vowels both plain and glottalized to their corresponding short "versions," e.g. *aa* becomes *a* or *a'a* becomes *a'*, depending on what follows. On the other hand, there are words that absolutely must be pronounced with interglottalized vowels and/or final *b*'s and *l*'s. My favorite example here is *ke'el* '(meteorological) cold'. If you say *kee* or *keel* or *ke'e*, you will not be understood or, if you are, you will be gently corrected. In the representation of Maya in this book, I have generally marked the glottal stops in vowels where most people pronounce them in careful speech, but often they are dropped in normal to rapid speech, and some speakers reject various glottalized pronunciations of many words in general. I have included final *b*'s and *l*'s even when they are regularly dropped at the end of words because the addition of a vowel suffix after them requires their pronunciation. You will also have to show a certain amount of tolerance for discrepancies between the way I represent Maya words in this book and what you actually hear from the Maya speakers you encounter. The watchword here is "go with the flow" and follow the practice of the native speakers you are with.

Stress and Intonation

This is a difficult subject because the basis of differentiation is really tone or pitch, not stress as in English and Spanish. The result is that Maya is spoken with a kind of "sing-song" quality. It is best learned by imitation. While there are a few examples where it can be used to differentiate meaning, it is not a prominent feature of the language, and so a beginner can carefully put it on the back burner in learning the language. A couple of crude generalizations may help, however. Generally, the pitch rises toward the end of the word. Either the last or the second to the last vowel is raised in many words, particularly inflected verb forms (see Chapter 4). Also, long vowels or at least some of them are often peaks in the words, even when they occur toward the beginnings of the words. It is possible to speak intelligible Maya without the pitch, and I have known gringos whose pitch was atrocious but whose Maya was otherwise good make themselves understood with no difficulty. But keep in mind that most Maya speakers have never heard anyone speak Maya as a foreign language. While English and Spanish speakers have adjusted to the variations encountered by listening to foreigners speak their languages, the Maya have not. Your having a horrendous accent when you pronounce Maya is just going to be one more reason for their not playing the game of helping the *ts'ulo'ob* (strangers) learn the language.

On the other hand, a reasonably competent pronunciation with even minimal halting Maya is apt to make you seem *simpático.*

The absolute worst pronunciation error is to "reduce" or change the quality of unstressed vowels like we do in English (e.g. 'telegraph' vs. 'telegraphy'). When in doubt, keep the intonation as flat and even as possible.

A Survey of Maya Alphabetic Representations

Modern Alphabet	Modern Variants	Colonial Alphabets[a]	Colonial Variants[a]
Vowels			
a		a	
e		e	
i		i	
o		o	
u		u	
Consonants			
b		b	
ch	c	ch	
ch'	c'	ch'	chh, chch, ch̄
h	j	h	
k		c	
k'		k	
l		l	
m		m	
n		n	
p		p	
p'		p'	pp, p
s		s	z, ç
t		t	
t'		t'	tt, th, ⱦ
ts	tz	tz	
ts'	dz, tz'	dz	ɔ
w		u	
x	š, sh	x	
y		y	

[a] Most representations in the Colonial alphabet run rough-shod over the glottalization and length of the vowels.

Phonetic Descriptions

Vowels

a:	low, back, unrounded vowel
e:	mid, front, unrounded vowel
i:	high, front, unrounded vowel
o:	mid, back, rounded vowel
u:	high, back, rounded vowel

Consonants

b:	voiced, glottalized bilabial stop
ch:	voiceless alveopalatal affricate
ch':	voiceless, glottalized alveopalatal affricate
h:	voiceless glottal glide or fricative
k:	voiceless velar stop
k':	voiceless, glottalized velar stop
l:	voiced lateral liquid
m:	voiced bilabial nasal
n:	voiced dental nasal
p:	voiceless bilabial stop
p':	voiceless, glottalized bilabial stop
r:	voiced sonorant lingual tap
s:	voiceless alveolar fricative
t:	voiceless dental stop
t':	voiceless, glottalized dental stop
ts:	voiceless alveolar affricate
ts':	voiceless, glottalized alveolar affricate
w:	voiced, rounded, high, back semi-vowel
x:	voiceless alveopalatal fricative
y:	voiced, unrounded, high, front semi-vowel

4. Grammar

The mere mention of the word 'grammar' is enough to strike terror into the hearts of many would-be language learners, and many language teaching methods crow that they make it possible to learn the language without learning the grammar. If you are someone who wants to avoid grammar, you may ignore this section and concentrate on overpowering the language by rote memorization of the phrases in Chapter 5 and of the vocabulary. You will, however, in the long run probably be making things more difficult for yourself. I hope that I can persuade you to at least try reading this section through a couple of times.

Grammar is merely an attempt to make generalizations about the structural patterns found in the language. Understanding *something* about the most basic patterns in Maya will help both in memorizing and understanding phrases and sentences, and it will enable you to make a reasonable attempt at putting things together to create new sentences and phrases out of the ones that you have already learned. I would be less than candid if I didn't tell you that Maya grammar is pretty heady stuff. For one thing, many of the "truths" of grammar that you may have come to assume as a result of learning English grammar and the grammars of other European languages turn out not to hold in Maya. In other words, the "logic" of the language is different. To make matters worse, the logic of Maya is not consequent in important cases, so that one kind of system is used for some constructions and another in others. I will try here to outline the most basic features of Maya grammar. It will probably be confusing to you because it is just a confusing system, or better, a set of systems.

I will try to simplify and generalize to make the description as tractable as possible. The price for that will be that what I say will sometimes, carried to its logical conclusion, turn out to be wrong. A very famous linguist who specialized in American Indian languages, Edward Sapir, said, "All grammars leak." By that standard, this sketch is little more than a sieve. In Chapter 7, I suggest some sources for more detailed and technical information on the language.

Sentence Structure

Our mindset from European languages tells us to worry about things like subjects and objects when we start to talk about sentences. While Maya does have subjects and objects and they do ultimately need to be identified, the best place to start is to think, rather simplemindedly, about a sentence in any language as a device for picking out things in the world and saying something about them. Let us call what we pick out to talk about the "topics" (there may be more than one) and what we say about them the "predication." Thus, in English the sentence

John is sleeping.

picks out 'John' as the topic and predicates of him that he is sleeping. The same pattern (but not necessarily the equivalent sentence) in Maya would be

Hwan tun wenel.

Here *Hwan* is the topic, and we predicate of him *tun wenel*, that he is sleeping. In Maya one can also say

Tun wenel Hwan.

In fact, this is more natural for Maya speakers than saying it with the English order. For the English,

John saw Peter.

in Maya one might say

Hwan tu yilah Pedro.

but one would more likely say

Tu yilah Pedro Hwan.

If you say

Tu yilah Hwan Pedro.

that is equivalent to

Peter saw John.

If in Maya you say

Binen Saki'.

the topic is *Saki'*, the Maya name for the city of Valladolid, and the predication is *binen* 'I went (there)', and so the sentence means 'I went to Valladolid'. You can also say

Saki' binen.

The difference between these last two sentences, and analogously the other pairs of Maya sentences above, is that when a topic precedes the predication it becomes "highlighted." The idea of highlighting in sentences is fairly elusive in English because it is often merely a matter of changing the sentence intonation slightly, but many other European languages do as Maya does and move highlighted phrases to the front of the sentence. The highlighted phrase is often the new information that the speaker brings to the discourse. Thus, by highlighting *Saki'*, the sentence could be the answer to the question *Tu'ux binech?* 'Where did you go?' One case where we can do something similar in English is with expressions of time, so that the word 'yesterday' can be placed at the beginning of an English sentence and thereby highlighted or it can be after the verb, in which case it is not highlighted.

A sentence may have several topics, e.g.,

Holyak binen Saki' yetel in watan.

Ho'lyak is 'yesterday' and *yetel in watan* is 'with my wife', and so the sentence means 'Yesterday I went to Valladolid with my wife.' Other permutations of the topics (*ho'lyak, Saki', yetel in watan*) with the predication (*binen*) are possible, but some are improbable, if not impossible.

There are a few basic principles to learn about the order of things. First, the predication generally goes close to the beginning of the sentence. If a topic comes before the predication, it is being highlighted or made important. Often it is the new information in the sentence. Second, if the sentence has both subject and object topics and they are after the predication, then the object precedes the subjects, as in the 'John saw Peter' sentences above.

The predication of a Maya sentence is usually a verb, or more generally a verb phrase, and the verb is easily the most complicated part of the language. It is also the most essential, and we will therefore begin our discussion with the verb.

Verb Forms

There are three basic verb forms (intransitive, transitive, and passive) and three aspects (completive, incompletive, and subjunctive). These two sets yield a total of nine possible combinations, but in the interest of keeping things simple, we will ignore for the time being the last member of each set (i.e. passive and subjunctive) and that will reduce the possible combinations to four.

In English, when we use a verb like 'eat', we can use it either transitively, i.e., with an overt object ('eat tortillas' or 'eat it') or we can use it intransitively, i.e., without an object. But either way the forms of 'eat' are the same: 'eats', 'ate', 'is eating', 'has eaten', etc. In Maya there is a single root *han* for 'eat', but the root must be incorporated into verb forms (words) that are either transitive or intransitive. Thus, *tin hanal* means 'I am eating', but *tin hantik* means 'I am eating it' or, with the object *waah* 'tortilla', *tin hantik waah* 'I am eating tortillas'. What is ungrammatical (not a well-formed sentence) in Maya would be **tin hanal waah*. (The asterisk is used to indicate that the construction is ungrammatical.)

While *hanal* and *hantik* are corresponding intransitive and transitive verbs, many verbs have only one form or the other. So, *wenel* 'sleep' occurs only intransitively, but *tuuxtik* 'send' occurs only transitively.

There are also two aspects for which Maya verbs are inflected. Aspects are a bit like tenses in English, but instead of dealing directly with time relations, they are used more broadly to show something about how the speaker views whatever he or she is talking about. One aspect, called "completive," is used to indicate that whatever the speaker is talking about is envisaged as a single act carried to completion. Normally, things that are done to completion happened in the past, and so completive constructions often wash out as English past. Thus, *Tin hantah le waaho'* would be 'I ate the tortilla.' The other aspect, "incompletive," is used in other situations including past ones if the activity is, say, repetitive or habitual. Thus, *Tin hantik waah* could be interpreted 'I was eating tortillas.' as well as 'I am eating tortillas.' habitually or at intervals.

As I said above, the intersection of the two aspects with the transitive/intransitive distinction yields four possible combinations, and we will discuss these forms in succession.

There are three basic elements in any verb form: the "verb stem" including some ending to differentiate transitivity and aspect, an "auxiliary" (usually), and one or two "pronominal affixes."

I will give the pronominal affixes first. There are two sets of affixes with different usages to be discussed presently. They distinguish person and number, like English or Spanish pronouns, but not gender (i.e., no 'he' vs. 'she'). The two sets are usually given the unilluminating names A and B. The A set is primarily prefixed, that is it goes in front of the stem, although the plural forms have two parts, one that goes on the front and another that goes on the rear. The technical name for such affixes is "ambifixes," if anybody cares. The first-person plural 'we' has several different possibilities which are not equivalent, but we will ignore differences now.

A Pronominal Affixes

	Singular	Plural
First person	*in*	*k*
		in —— o'on
		k —— e'ex
Second person	*a*	*a —— e'ex*
Third person	*u*	*u —— o'ob*

Note: The three different first-person plural forms (English 'we') are confusing. The basic form is the first one listed, *k*. In some parts of the Zona Maya (central Quintana Roo) and in the adjacent parts of northern Quintana Roo and eastern Yucatan, the *in ——o'on,* an analogical development from the other plural forms of the singular pronominal prefix and the B pronominal suffix (see below), is used in some (but not all) situations where an A affix is used. The third form, *k ——e'ex,* has a different meaning. It is used when 'we' means more than one person being addressed, sort of 'you all and I'. Many speakers do not use it consistently, however. You have to pay attention to what people use and try to imitate their practice, but messing it up is not catastrophic. You will probably be understood in any case.

When the *in, a,* or *u* pronominal affixes are followed by a stem beginning with a vowel, the stem gets either *w-* prefixed to it after *in* or *a* or *y-* prefixed to it after the *u*. Since the prefixed *y-* unambiguously signals third person, the *u* may be optionally dropped.

The B set of pronouns are exclusively suffixed to verb stems.

B Pronominal Affixes

	Singular	Plural
First person	*-en*	*-o'on*
Second person	*-ech*	*-e'ex*
Third person	*(-i)*	*-o'ob*

Note: The third-person singular ending is in parenthesis because the suffix is technically not a pronominal affix but rather a phrase marker (see Phrase and Discourse Markers, below). It usually appears only when the pronoun marks the subject and the verb is the last word in the sentence. If another phrase, e.g., a subject topic, follows, then there is no affix at all on the verb for the third-person singular here.

Incompletive Intransitives

An incompletive may consist of simply a pronominal affix on a verb stem, but these are relatively unusual. Most of the time there is also an auxiliary involved which then appears as the first element in the verb phrase followed by the A pronoun and then the verb stem. There is a fairly extensive set of auxiliaries, but for starters we will use one example *k*, which is used in habitual, general, and generic statements (more on that later). Our old friend *hanal* 'eat' would look like the following:

kin hanal 'I eat'   *k hanal(e'ex)/kin hanalo'on*
                                    'we eat'
ka hanal 'you eat'   *ka hanale'ex* 'you (all) eat'
ku hanal 's/he eats'   *ku hanalo'ob* 'they eat'

An example of an incompletive intransitive stem beginning with a vowel (remember the *w/y* business above) is *eemel* 'go down, descend':

kin weemel 'I descend'   *k eemel(e'ex)/kin weemelo-*
                                    'on 'we descend'
ka weemel 'you descend'   *ka weemele'ex* 'you (all)
                                    descend'
ku yeemel 's/he descends'   *ku yeemelo'ob* 'they descend'

Incompletive Transitives

Like the incompletive intransitives, these forms typically also include an auxiliary. As an example here we will use the same auxiliary, but as a verb we will use *hats'ik* 'hit, strike':

kin hats'ik 'I hit it/him/her'   *k hats'ik(e'ex)* 'we hit it/him/
                                    her'
                                    kin hats'ko'on

ka hats'ik 'you hit it/him/   *ka hats'ke'ex* 'you hit it/him/
    her'   her'
ku hats'ik 's/he hits it/him/   *ku hats'ko'ob* 'they hit it/
    her'   him/her'

As you can see, with no overt object the transitive verbs are interpreted as having an object 'it' or 'him' or 'her'. It is, of course, possible to simply add a name or noun phrase as the object, e.g., *Kin hats'ik Hwan.* 'I hit John.', *Ku hats'ik le pak'o'.* 'S/he hits the wall.' In addition, one can add the B pronouns (except *-i*) to the end of the forms above, subject to two restrictions: (1) just as in English, there can be no overlapping reference, e.g., *'I hit me' or *'I hit us' and (2) only one *-o'ob* to a form, e.g., not *ku hats'ko'obo'ob* 'they hit them' but rather *ku hats'ko'ob*. Some examples are *kin hats'kech* 'I hit you', *ka hats'ken* 'you hit me', etc.

Completive Intransitives

These forms generally use no auxiliary but, to make things that much worse, they use the B pronouns *to show the subject.* The *-al* or similar ending of the incompletive intransitive (e.g. *hanal*) is not present in these forms. The completive aspect means something done once to completion, and it washes out usually as the past tense in English. However, the reverse is not true because the English past tense can have several other meanings such as something done repeatedly in the past. Also, completive in the future is possible. Here are the forms:

hanen 'I ate'   *hano'on* 'we ate'
hanech 'you ate'   *hane'ex* 'you ate'
hani 's/he ate'   *hano'ob* 'they ate'

Note the single ending on the third-person singular.

Completive Transitives

This form adds *-ah* instead of *-ik* at the end of the stem and uses the auxiliary *t-* which combines with the A pronouns.

tin hats'ah 'I hit it'   *t hats'ah(e'ex)* 'we hit it'
                                       tin hats'aho'on

ta hats'ah 'you hit it'   *ta hats'ahe'ex* 'you hit it'
tu hats'ah 's/he hit it'   *tu hats'aho'ob* 'they hit it'

As with the incompletive transitives, the B pronouns may be added as objects: *tin hats'ahech* 'I hit you', *ta hats'ahen* 'you hit me', etc., subject to the usual restrictions.

Special Classes of Verbs

As do most languages, Maya has different patterns for conjugating verbs, but the patterns that have been presented above are the most widespread and general in the language. A brief description of a couple of important variants of the intransitive patterns should be helpful, however. First, there are a substantial number of intransitives which do not use the *-Vl* ending in the incompletive (where *V* is a cover symbol for whatever the vowel of the noun stem is; this repetition is called "vowel harmony") but are otherwise conjugated like those intransitives shown above. This would be a minor wrinkle, except that exactly these verbs add a suffix to the stem before any B-pronominal affixes. The suffix is based on a consonant followed by *ah*. The most common consonant is *n*, and so *-nah* is the most common of these completive intransitive suffixes. When intransitive verbs are borrowed from Spanish (the infinitive is always the form borrowed), this pattern is always used. For example, 'win' in Spanish is *ganar*, and so *ganarnahen* would be Maya for 'I won'.

There are two common apparent exceptions to these patterns: *bin* 'go' and *tal* 'come', as they take neither the *-Vl* in the incompletive, e.g., *tin bin* 'I am going' (not *tin binil), nor *-nah* in the completive *talen* 'I came' (not *talnahen). The explanation is that historically they did take the *-Vl* suffix but lost it relatively recently.

Another important subclass of intransitives are those ending in the suffix *-tal* in the incompletive. Often they express a meaning of becoming or getting to some state or condition. For example, *kaltal* means 'get drunk' and *nohochtal* means 'become big'. In the completive the *-tal* suffix is replaced with *-chah* to which the B-pronominal affixes are added, e.g. *kalchahech* 'you got drunk'.

It is also worth knowing how transitive verbs are borrowed from Spanish. The infinitive simply has a *-t* suffix added to it followed by either of the usual transitive aspect suffixes -*ik* or -*ah*. For example, Spanish *seguir* is used in Maya as *segirtik* to mean 'continue'.

Auxiliaries

There is a fairly wide variety of auxiliaries which can be used with the incompletive verb forms, both transitive and intransitive. We list here some of the most important with examples. Remember, the A pronoun as subject always immediately follows the auxiliary. For a few very important auxiliaries the following pronoun is "contracted" with the auxiliary to give a "special" form, just like in English, where 'can not' contracts as 'can't'. The contraction in Maya is somewhat idiosyncratic, just like 'will' and 'not' contract as 'won't' and not *'willn't' and 'may' and 'not' for many English-speakers don't contract at all ('mayn't').

tan   This auxiliary is used to talk about activities which are seen as processes; it washes out as something like the progressive forms in English. It may (but doesn't have to) contract in the following ways: *tan in = tin, tan a = tan, tan u = tun*, and *tan k = tank* (the last is obligatory), for example: *Tin hantik waah.* 'I'm eating tortillas.', *Tank bin Saki'.* 'We're going to Valladolid.', *Tun wenel Hwan.* 'John's sleeping.'

k   This was used in the examples introducing the aspectual system, so it is not necessary to go over the forms here again. Its meaning is also the most elusive of all the auxiliaries. One way to look at it is as a kind of "default" auxiliary, one to put in when others don't seem right. A couple of usages should be mentioned, however. One is that it is quite common in questions, particularly those that ask for information. Two of the standard greeting questions use this auxiliary and can be used to illustrate: *Tu'ux ka bin?* literally 'Where do you go?' and *Ba'ax ka wa'alik?* 'What do you say?' The second use is for sentences that describe habitual or repeated action, e.g., *Ku konik si' Hwan.* 'John sells firewood.'

ma'   This is the negative particle and can be used, among other ways, as an auxiliary. It may be contracted with *in* as *min*, *a* as *ma'*, and *u* as *mu'*. Negative sentences also end with an -*i'*, so it's probably better to think of *ma'* ——-*i'* as a kind of "dance team" that always goes together, for example *Min wohli'.* 'I don't know.', *Mu'k'ahoteni'.* 'S/he doesn't recognize me.'

taak   This auxiliary expresses desire and does not contract. One usage is example *Taak in kanik le mayao'.* 'I want to learn Maya.'

hop'/hok   This is an inceptive auxiliary meaning to initiate or begin some activity. It can also be used, with appropriate endings, as a regular verb. As an example of its use as an auxiliary, consider the following: *Hop' u hanal.* 'S/he is beginning to eat.' The form *hok* is a variant used in Quintana Roo.

k'abeet   This auxiliary indicates necessity and therefore glosses out as 'need', e.g., *K'abeet in wantik le nohoch maako'.* 'I gotta help the old man.'

yan   This also expresses necessity, but more weakly than *k'abeet,* and is more associated with volition or intention. As such, it is frequently simply the expression of future time for the activity described. So, *Yan in wantik le nohoch maako'.* is more like 'I'm going to help the old man.' or 'I should help the old man.' *Yan* also has a "past" form (actually it's completive), *yanhi,* and this when used as an auxiliary is equivalent to English 'had to' or Spanish *tenía que.* Therefore, *Yanhi in wantik le nohoch maako'.* is 'I had to help the old man.'

ts'ook   This is the terminative auxiliary and focuses attention on the end or completion of some activity: *Ts'ook in hanal.* 'I'm done eating.', *Ts'ook in k'aatik.* 'I've already asked for it.' (cf. Spanish *ya ordené*). You may be a bit nonplussed by the fact *ts'ook* is used with incompletive verb forms because it appears to defy the basic meaning distinction between the completive and non-completive aspects. There are two ways to deal with this. One is to simply accept the fact that this is the way things work in Maya. The other is to remember that the completive focuses on the whole activity, not just its termination. Contractions of *ts'ook* with the singular A pronouns as *ts'in, ts'a,* and *ts'u* and *ts'ook* (with *k* 'we') are also possible.

Stative Verbs

As their name indicates, they are used to express states, but not all things that express states are stative verbs. There are plenty of regular intransitive verbs that express a state, e.g., *tun wenel* 's/he is sleeping'. Stative verbs are largely equivalent to adjectives in English or Spanish, but with the important difference that they don't need "helping verbs" and that sort of thing; rather, they can be used to form sentences all by themselves. For example, *ke'el* is a stative verb meaning 'cold' (of weather only), and so it can also be translated 'it's cold'. Even nouns can be used as stative verbs, and *winik* 'man' can be used as a sentence to mean 'He's a man.' Many stative verbs can have a topic associated with them. Thus, using the stative verb *k'oha'an* 'sick' to say 'John is sick', we can say something like *k'oha'an Hwan* or *Hwan k'oha'an*. To talk about 'I', 'you', 'we', etc., the appropriate B pronoun is added to the end, e.g., *k'oha'nen* 'I am sick.' Analogously, *ke'elen* means 'I'm cold' and *winken* 'I am a man.' Use of these words as nouns and adjectives in noun phrases, i.e. topic constructions, will be described below.

Reflexive Verbs

Maya also has some verbs that are reflexive like Spanish. Basically they are transitive but add an affix *-ba* that itself takes A pronouns that agree with the subject of the verb. As an example, let us look at the verb for 'approach' or 'draw near' in Maya, *naats'kuba*. The stem is *naats'*, which has the basic meaning 'near'. The *k* is the remains of the transitive suffix *-ik* with the *i* deleted. The *u* is the third-person A pronominal affix (used in the citation form of the verb) and the *-ba* is the reflexive. The conjugation of the incompletive is as follows:

tin naats'kimba 'I am approaching'
tan naats'kaba 'you are approaching'
tun naats'kuba 's/he is approaching'

tank naats'kba(e'ex)/tin naats'kimbao'on 'we are approaching'
tan naats'kabae'ex 'you are approaching'
tun naats'kubao'ob 'they are approaching'

Reflexives in Maya may be idiosyncratic as in Spanish (for example, *acercarse*, the Spanish equivalent of *naats'kuba*) or show identity of subject and object as in English.

Noun Phrases

Noun phrases are the major items used as sentence topics in Maya. The central element in a noun phrase is, not surprisingly, a noun.

Additional elements in a noun phrase can be said to modify the noun. The most basic set of noun modifiers is the determiners, which is a fancy name for articles and other things that can be substituted for articles, such as possessives ('my' and 'your', in English) and demonstratives ('this', 'that', etc.).

The only change that can be made in nouns is to make them plural, like in English or Spanish. There are no case markers, as in many languages. Like English and Spanish, Maya adds a single suffix to nouns to make them plural, namely -o'ob, with a very small residual number of "irregular" plurals. An example would be *che'o'ob* 'trees', the plural of *che'* 'tree'. To say 'the tree' you put *le* in front of the noun and the suffix -o' on the end of the noun, so that *le che'o'* would be 'the tree'. This works equally well with plural nouns yielding *le che'o'obo'* 'the trees'. If we use -a' as the suffix instead of -o', the result is the equivalent of 'this, these', e.g. *le che'a'* 'this tree', *le che'o'oba'* 'these trees'.

For the indefinite article, 'a(n)' in English, Maya uses the number 'one', just like Spanish. The numbers also use classifiers (see Noun Phrase Modifiers), and the numeral stem *hun-* 'one' attached to the appropriate classifier *kul* gives *hunkul*, which placed before the noun gives us *hunkul che'* 'a tree'. Indefinite plurals have no article, just as in English and Spanish, e.g., *che'o'ob* 'trees' (in general).

Although plural can be marked with the -o'ob suffix as shown, it is important to note that it is not marked when the fact that there is more than one is obvious from the context. For example, if a flock of turkeys is blocking the road and the driver wants to identify why he has stopped the vehicle, he would say to the passengers *Uulum!* not *Uulmo'ob!* where in English or Spanish one would say 'Turkeys!' or ¡Pavos! Tortillas are almost always *waah*, as in *Tin hantik waah.* 'I am eating tortillas.' not *waaho'ob* because the activity involves an indefinite number of tortillas but certainly more than one. After numbers and quantifiers (see the following section), nouns are usually not inflected for plural.

The A pronominal affixes that you learned for the verbs are also used with nouns to show possession. In addition the suffix -*il* or -*Vl may* be added to a noun. So for the word *nah* 'house', *in nahil* is 'my house', *a nahile'ex* 'your (pl.) house', and so forth. A couple of special rules apply. First, the -*il*/-*Vl* suffix, if present, goes before any other suffix. The plural suffix precedes the -*e'ex* part of the plural ambifixes, e.g., *a nahilo'obe'ex* 'your (*pl.*) houses'. Finally, there can only be one *-o'ob* suffix present so that *u nahilo'ob* can be 'his/her houses', 'their house' or 'their houses'! An example with vowel harmony is *kaah* 'town', which becomes *in kaahal* 'my town'.

Some nouns, namely terms for body parts and relatives, are always possessed. When talking about the word, the 'your' form is used, e.g., *a ni'* 'your nose', *a tata* 'your father'.

When a name or a descriptive noun phrase is named as the possessor of something, the possessed object has the form for 'his/her/its' possession, i.e., *u* in front of it and possibly *-il/-Vl* as a suffix, and the possessor usually follows. Thus, *nah* 'house' becomes *u nahil* 'his/her/its house', which becomes *u nahil Hwan* 'John's house'. This also is used for the equivalent of 'of'-type expressions in English, e.g. *chumuk* 'middle' becomes *u chumuk* 'its middle' and *u chumuk le kaaho'* 'the middle of the town' (literally, 'its middle the town').

Prepositions

There is only one all-purpose preposition, *ti'*, in Maya, which indicates general direction or location, i.e. 'to, from, in, on, at', etc. When it is followed by *le* (the article), *in, a,* or *u* (the pronominal affixes, typically in their possessive function), they contract as *te, tin, ta,* and *tu* respectively, e.g., *te kaaho'* 'to the town'. For *ti'* with first- and second-person pronominal objects (e.g. 'to me', 'to you', 'to us'), forms that look like contractions of *ti'* with the B pronominal affixes are used. These forms have another use, however, and so they are called the C pronouns, which are shown here.

C Pronouns

	Singular	Plural
First person	*ten*	*to'on*
Second person	*tech*	*te'ex*
Third person	*leeti'*	*leeti'o'ob*

The third-person forms are not used with *ti'*, so to express 'to him/her/it', you just use *ti'* with nothing after it, which means this will be clause final (see Phrase and Discourse Markers, below) and therefore get an *-e* tacked on to it, i.e., *ti'e.* The plural is *ti'o'ob(e).*

The regular use of the C pronouns (including *leeti', leeti'o'ob*) is when you want to have a pronoun as a sentence topic. In this use they typically appear in the highlighted-topic position in front of the predication. Thus, *Ten tin bin* is something like 'I'm the one who is going.' where just *Tin bin* is 'I'm going.'

Actually that's about like Spanish (cf. *yo me voy* vs. *me voy*).

Back to prepositions. Other things that are equivalent to English or Spanish prepositional phrases are constructed around nouns, some of which are seldom or never used in isolation. Let's look at an example. The noun *et* probably means something like 'accompaniment' or 'instrumentality' (see examples in the glossary), but hooked up with a possessor name or noun phrase it sprouts a *u* followed by a *y* attached to *et* (remember the rule about A pronominal affixes before stems beginning with a vowel) and a *-Vl* suffix, yielding a theoretical **u yetel.* Remember, however, that the *y* prefixed to the noun makes the *u* redundant. Usually dropping the *u* is optional, but here it must go, yielding *yetel.* With a possessor name or noun phrase after it, we get *yetel Hwan* 'the accompaniment of John' or simply 'with John'. In 95 percent of the cases you could just say *yetel* is the preposition 'with', and you put the object after it. However, with the first- and second-person pronoun forms, the truth that we ultimately have a possessed noun is seen in the forms: *tin wetel, ta wetel, ta wetele'ex, tek etelo'on* or *tin wetelo'on.* Note that these forms also begin with *ti',* appropriately contracted with the following pronoun. Other forms equivalent to prepositions work the same way: *ti'al* 'for', *yok'ol* 'over, above' (the nominal root is **ok'*), *yaanal* 'under' (root ** aan*).

Still other nouns used to form expressions equivalent to English and Spanish prepositional phrases require the "real" preposition *ti'* at the beginning of the phrase, e.g., *tu tsel le naho'* 'beside the house' (literally, 'at its side the house'). The noun *chumuk* 'middle' works the same way to form an expression of location, e.g., *tu chumuk le k'aaxo'* 'in/to the middle of the jungle'. A particularly important and frequent set of constructions is built around a noun *iknal* that, if it occurred in isolation, would mean something like 'one's space' in the sense that this term is used in pop psychology. Thus, the expression *tin wiknal* means 'at my house, where I am', or is perhaps best translated by the French *chez moi.*

The final preposition we need to mention is *ich(il)* 'in(side)'. The short form *ich* is used with nouns without any modifiers such as in the fixed expression *ich kol* 'in his milpa' and with languages, e.g., *ich maya* 'in Maya'. Unlike the noun-based prepositional collocations beginning with vowels, *ichil* never takes the *y-* or *w-* prefix. Also, it doesn't take the A pronominal prefixes for the various first- and second-person forms. The way to say 'inside (of) me' in Maya is *ichil ti' ten*.

Noun Phrase Modifiers

The stative verbs mentioned above can generally also be used as modifiers within a noun phrase. The natural position in Maya for such modifiers is before the noun, like in English. For example, the word *nohoch* 'big, large' can be introduced into the noun phrase *le che'o'* 'the tree' to yield *le nohoch che'o'* 'the big tree'. The modifiers generally do not change to "agree" with the noun in any way. The single exception here is *nohoch,* which has a special plural form *nukuch,* e.g., *le nukuch che'o'obo'* 'the big trees'. Maya also lacks a native system for expressing direct comparison. The Spanish *más* has been borrowed for such purposes, e.g., *le che'o' mas nohoch.* Often the intensifier *hach* 'very' is used for expression of comparison and is a lot like the *-ísimo* ending in Spanish, e.g., *le hach nukuch che'o'obo'* 'los árboles grandísimos'.

Another important class of noun phrase modifiers is the quantifiers, i.e., those expressions used to express amounts. Here we can start with *ya'ab,* which means 'a lot' or 'much', e.g., *ya'ab ha'* 'a lot of water'. When the amount is countable, the form *ya'abkach* 'many' is also used, e.g., *ya'abkach maak(o'ob)* 'a lot of people'. The noun may or may not be in its plural form, which is after all redundant. The distinction between *ya'ab* with mass nouns and *ya'abkach* with count nouns is generally ignored in Maya, and expressions like *ya'ab maak* 'many people' are used all the time. A useful analogy can be made with the way the distinction between 'less' and 'fewer' is ignored in English, and 'less calories' is used even in advertising.

The use of singular noun forms is also characteristic after numbers as well. The native numbers are used only up to 'four' by most Maya today. Numbers also are almost always used with classifiers, i.e., suffixes or "counting words" to which the number stem is attached. There were in earlier times dozens of different classifiers which were used to talk about given classes of items, some of them quite specific. If you want to learn about the now-extinct counting system of Classical Maya, look at Tozzer, pp. 96–104 and 290–292 (see Chapter 7). Of course, there are some Maya, almost all better-educated city dwellers, who know the higher numeration and some or all of the classifiers because they got a book and learned them. The following is all that is really in use now:

> Number stems: *hun-* 'one', *ka'-* 'two', *ox-* 'three', *kan-* 'four'.
> Classifiers: *-p'el* 'non-living things', *-tul* 'animals and human beings', *-ts'it* 'long, slender objects', *-kul* 'trees'.

It should be pointed out that even the classifier system given here is in decline, and many people simply use *-p'el* with all inanimate objects (thereby avoiding the specialized classifiers *-ts'it* and *-kul*) and many animate and even human nouns such as Spanish borrowings, e.g., *oxp'el ermanos* 'three brothers'. Also the *-p'el* form is used when talking about numbers or counting.

When *hun-* and *kan-* are joined with *-p'el*, the *n* at the end of the stem changes to *m*, e.g. *hump'el, kamp'el*.

An additional classifier with a special meaning is *-hul*. Used with *ka'-*, *ox-*, and *kan-*, it means 'identical', e.g., *ka'hul suum* 'two identical ropes'. Sometimes the Spanish numbers are combined with Mayan ones in order to get the classifier in front of a Maya noun, e.g., *seys huntul u maak* 'six people' or *siyete hump'ele waah* 'seven tortillas'. Nouns may be either singular or plural after numbers above one.

Expressing 'Have' in Maya

There is no verb in Maya like 'have' in English or *tener* in Spanish. In English we use 'have' to inquire about availability, e.g. 'Do you have any eggs?' In Maya, as in Spanish, one asks about existence to mean availability. In Spanish ¿*hay huevos*? is the way to ask about availability of eggs. In Maya likewise the existential predicate *yan* 'there is/are' is used to ask, e.g., *yan he'*?, the answer to which is either *yan* 'there are' or *mina'an* 'there are no(ne)'. A widely utilized colloquial alternative to *mina'an* is *na'am*, and so you have to get used to hearing and using both.

In expressing true possession, *yan* is used together with a C pronoun or *ti'(o'ob)* in the third person for alienable possessible, i.e. things that you can dispose of by sale, abandonment, loss, etc., or with the possessed form of inalienably possessed nouns, e.g. relatives and body parts. For example, to ask if someone has money, you could say *Yan tech taak'in?* to which the possible answers are *yan* (yes) or *mina'an* or *na'am* (no). Or to ask if someone has an older brother *Yan a suku'un?* with the same answers.

Talking about Movement

The way the Maya talk about movement involves a set of verbs that define certain parameters. For example, one parameter is the direction of the movement, which is either away from or toward what is seen as a site of the description. This is quite familiar to you from English because it is exactly the difference between 'go' and 'come', which are the glosses for the Mayan verbs *bin* and *tal* respectively. The direction is incorporated into the verb so that no preposition is used to specify it. The question *Tu'ux ka bin?* 'Where are you going?' is answered with no preposition when using a place name, e.g., *Tin bin Saki'.* Likewise, the *Tu'ux talech?* literally 'Where did you come?' gets the answer *Talen Saki'.* literally 'I came Valladolid.' In fact, while Maya has a couple of prepositions that can be interpreted as expressing motion toward, like 'to' or 'toward' in English, there is nothing remotely resembling 'from' except *deste* which is used sometimes from Spanish. When common descriptions of places rather than place names or deictic expression (i.e., 'here' and 'there') are used, the all-purpose preposition *ti'* must be added, e.g., *Tin bin tin nahil.* 'I am going to my house.' or *Talen tin kaahal.* 'I came to my (home)town.' A third basic verb of motion *maan* expresses neither direction toward or away, and so it is like 'pass' in English. A sentence like *Maanen Saki'.* is like 'I passed through/by Valladolid.'

There is also a pair of verbs which emphasizes the inception of motion. The verb *hook'ol* means to start out with motion toward, like *salir* in Spanish, while *luk'ul* is starting out with motion away, like Spanish *quitar*. Motion into a closed or defined space is expressed by *okol* 'enter'. The termination of motion is expressed by *k'uchul* and is neutral with respect to direction like its English gloss 'arrive'.

Vertical movement is expressed by the verbs *na'akal* for upward, like Spanish *subirse,* and *eemel* for downward, like Spanish *bajarse.* The Spanish glosses are much more helpful in determining usage than is English, in which these movements are expressed by a range of collocations like 'get up', 'get on', 'climb (up)', 'ascend', etc., for upward motion and corresponding terms for downward.

Virtually all of the roots of the verbs of motion occur suffixed by the causative suffix *-s* followed by the transitive suffixes of aspect (i.e., *-ik* and *-ah*) which have meanings something like 'cause something or someone to move in the particular way', which is roughly what 'bring' and 'take' are in English. Thus the most general verbs of motion, *bin* 'go' and *tal* 'come', are reformed as *bi(n)sik* 'take' and *taa(l)sik* 'bring'. The root-final consonants, *n* and *l* respectively, are never used in these words in modern Maya. Other examples of transitive verbs of motion are *mansik* 'carry' (i.e., cause something to pass by), *oksik* 'insert' (i.e. cause something to enter), and *ensik* 'lower' (i.e. cause something to descend). While these words are best learned as expressions for the corresponding English and Spanish terms when learning Maya, understanding the basis of the word formation can facilitate memorization.

Making Requests

The forms for making requests in Maya are quite straightforward but different for transitive and intransitive verbs respectively. Transitive verbs use simply the stem of the verb with any aspectual suffix (e.g., *-ik*) taken off. Thus, for *taasik* 'bring' you remove the suffix and say, for example, *Taas ten hump'el boxha'.* 'Bring me a (cup of) coffee.' If the stem ends with a cluster of consonants that is difficult to pronounce, an *e* may be added to facilitate pronunciation, e.g., *hante* 'eat it' (from *hantik*), *chupes* 'fill it' (from *chupsik*).

With intransitives, any suffix (e.g., *-al*) is removed and the imperative suffix *-en* is added. For the verb *hanal* 'eat', the request (or command) form is *Hanen!* 'Eat!' The two basic motion verbs *bin* 'go' and *tal* 'come' have irregular request or command forms: *xen* and *ko'oten*, respectively. All command forms may be pluralized by adding the suffix *-e'ex*, e.g., *ko'otene'ex.*

Questions

Requests for information in English involve the use of a special set of words called either "interrogative pronouns" or, perhaps a better mnemonic, "*wh*-words" because all but one (*how*) begin with the letter combination *wh*. The important Maya words corresponding to these mostly end in *x*, and so we can call them "*x*-words." The most important *x*-words are: *ba'ax* 'what', *maax* 'who', *biix* 'how', *tu'ux* 'where', *makalmak* 'which' (doesn't end in *x*), and *kuux* (see below). Their use is quite easy because, like in English and Spanish, they are placed at the beginning of the sentence. They are also used alone like in English and Spanish to ask eliptical questions which are understood by the discourse context in which they are used, e.g., Spanish ¿*Quien*? 'Who?' In Maya when used this way, a discourse marker (see below) is often added so that the equivalent question in Maya is *Maaxi'?*, which is *maax* 'who' with the suffix *-i'*. Maya also has one *x*-word for which English uses a collocation, and that is *kuux*. This word is used to ask the same question a second time about a different person or object. If, for example, a waiter asks one person in a group *Ba'ax taak a hantik?* 'What do you want to eat?' and takes that person's order, he will turn to the next person and say *Kuux tech?* The English equivalent is 'how about', and so *Kuux tech?* means 'How about you?'

There is also a particle *wa* which can be inserted in a sentence in a position other than at the beginning of the sentence to make the sentence a yes-no question, e.g., *Binech wa Saki'?* 'Did you go to Valladolid?' Apparently in earlier times questions in Maya were spoken without a rising intonation as is done in English and Spanish, but the influence of Spanish has now made the use of rising intonation in questions pervasive. As a consequence the most common way to make yes-no questions is simply to give them rising intonation so that *Binech Saki'?* is a more colloquial version of the same question.

Other Verb Forms

As I said at the beginning there are three aspects and three voices for the verbs which yield nine possible forms for any verb. I outlined the mechanics of the four most important combinations: intransitive incompletive, transitive incompletive, intransitive completive, and transitive completive. This is not to say that the remaining aspect (subjunctive) and voice (passive) are not useful. To know Maya well and use it properly, you've to master subjunctive and passive forms, just like with any European language. Some of the expressions given in the phrase and vocabulary sections of this book use subjunctive or passive forms simply because they are the correct ones. But if you mess up the subjunctive, you will probably still be intelligible. With the passive there is, of course, the potentially serious problem of confusing who is the actor and who is the receiver of the action which the passive "reverses," more or less like in English. Nevertheless, the practical chances of having a major misunderstanding are pretty slim.

Below, all the first-person singular verb forms are presented in tabular form followed by a descriptive analysis for reference purposes, but remember that I haven't given you any usage rules for the subjunctive. They are fairly extensive and do not correspond to, say, Spanish subjunctive, so don't expect too much from this.

First-Person Singular Verb Forms

Aspect

Form	Completive	Incompletive	Subjunctive
Intransitive	han-*en*	(tan) *in* han-*al*	han-*ak-en*
Transitive	*t-in* hant-*ah*	(tan) *in* hant-*ik*	*in* hante
Passive	hant-*ab-en*	(tan) *in* hant-*a'al*	hant-*a'ak-en*

Analysis of Forms

- The intransitive completive consists of the intransitive verb base (*han*) with a B pronoun (*-en*) suffixed to indicate the subject.
- The intransitive incompletive consists of the intransitive verb base (*han*) optionally preceded by an auxiliary (*tan*) followed by an A pronoun (*in*), which may be suffixed to or contracted with

the auxiliary (e.g., *tin*). The stem is followed by the suffix *-Vl*, where the harmony principle applies: *V* is the vowel that is the stem of the verb.base if the base is simple, otherwise *V* = *a*.

- The intransitive subjunctive consists of the intransitive verb base (*han*) followed by the suffix *-Vk*, with the harmony principle determining *V*, which is in turn followed by a B pronominal suffix (*-en*) except in the third-person singular.

- The transitive completive consists of the mandatory auxiliary *t-* to which an A pronominal affix (*in*) is attached to reflect the subject. This is followed by the transitive verb stem followed by the suffix *-ah*. B pronominal suffixes, if required, are suffixed as object pronouns to the result.

- The transitive incomplete begins with the optional auxiliary (*tan*) followed by an A pronominal affix (*in*) appropriately attached to or contracted with the auxiliary (e.g., *tin*). This is followed by the transitive verb stem (*hant*) to which the suffix *-ik* is attached. B pronominal suffixes are suffixed as objects, if required, to the result.

- The transitive subjunctive consists of an A pronominal affix (*in*) preceding the transitive verb stem (*hant*), with B pronominal suffixes, if required, suffixed as object pronouns.

- The passive completive uses the suffix *-ab* attached to the transitive verb stem (*hant*) to which B pronominal forms (*-en*) are suffixed as subjects.

- The passive incomplete has an optional auxiliary (*tan*) followed by an A pronominal affix (*in*) preceding the transitive verb stem (*hant*) with the suffix *-a'al*.

- The passive subjunctive consists of the transitive verb stem (*hant*) followed by the suffix *-a'ak* with B pronominal forms (*-en*) suffixed to the result.

Phrase and Discourse Markers

Maya has a dicey system of using suffixes to mark various things in sentences. You saw a little bit of this above when the "dance team" of *le* together with *-o'* or *-a'* sandwiching a noun is equivalent to things like 'the', 'this', and 'that', e.g., *le pek'o'oba'* 'these dogs'. Obviously, any modifying adjectives are also framed by the two markers, e.g., *le nukuch pek'o'obo'* 'those big dogs'. Because the markers appear at both edges of a noun phrase, clauses can also be framed and made relative, e.g., *le pek' tin wilaho'* 'the dog that I saw.'

Another "dance team" mentioned above was the negative *ma'* with the suffix *-i'*, e.g., *ma' in wohli'* 'I don't know' (*min wohli'*). This frames what it sometimes called the "scope" of the negation.

The *-i'* suffix is also tacked onto the end of question words when they are used alone. *Ba'ax* is the word for 'what', but if you want to ask 'What is it?' you are supposed to say *Ba'axi'*? However, the suffix is not used when a word follows the question word, e.g., *Ba'ax lelo'*? 'What's that?'

There is also the suffix *-e'*. It can be added to a topic appearing before a verb and has the effect of "focusing" that topic. It is used, for example, when one wants to switch back to talking about someone or something which had been mentioned much earlier. So let's go back to the first Maya sentence in this grammar:

Hwan tun wenel.

'John is sleeping.' If you put the suffix on 'John', you get

   Hwane' tun wenel.

which in English would be something like 'As for John, he's sleeping.'

There are also similar suffixes *-i* and *-e*, without glottal stops, which are used as "terminals," which is to say that they are placed at the end of sentences ending with certain forms when nothing else is there. The final *-e* after the preposition *ti'* (e.g., *ti'e* 'to him/her/it') and the final *-i* after completive intransitives (e.g., *bini* 'he went', but *bin Hwan* 'John went') described in the grammar are examples of such usage. To some extent these suffixes are like verbal punctuation marks. You should be aware of them when listening to Maya speakers, but you don't need to be overly concerned with the subtleties of using them when speaking Maya yourself because they are not crucial to your being understood.

5. How to Talk about Things

In this section I have attempted to describe how you talk with Maya-speaking people about their world and your visit to it. It is organized by subject areas, as are many phrase books for travelers. The problem is, of course, that you have no way of knowing what kind of verbal responses you might evoke by using such phrases. Fortunately, traditional Maya people tend to be rather circumspect in talking to *ts'ulo'ob* (strangers), so that answers and responses are usually reasonably short and often fairly transparent.

It is important to keep in mind that you can really best use the language to talk about their traditional world, not yours or even those parts of their world that are not traditional. There are many things for which one must use either individual Spanish words or even entire sentences. The technical name for mixing two languages is code-switching, you will remember, and although purists abhor "Spanglish" and other kinds of code-switching, it is pretty much a fact of life in speaking Maya, particularly as an outsider.

First Things

One of the most basic things is what to say when encountering someone. The Maya know and use the Spanish greetings *ola* (Spanish *hola*) and *bwenas* (Spanish *buenas*) with or without the various endings (*días, tardes, noches*). Note that many Maya say *bwenas* (and not *buenos*) *días*. A more traditional expression, one that assumes that the person greeted is not a total stranger, although not merely an acquaintance, is *Tu'ux ka bin?* 'Where are you going?' Using this is appropriate only when the person is obviously under way somewhere. Similarly, one can use *Biix a beel?* 'How are things with you?' and *Ba'ax ka wa'alik?* 'What do you say?' The formulaic response to the first is *ma'aloob* 'o.k., fine', and either *mixba'al* 'nothing' or *chen beya'* 'only this' to the latter.

One of the things that people want to learn first in any language are the expressions associated with politeness ('please', 'thank you', 'would you be so kind', etc.). The tradition of having baroque systems for expressing those kinds of things is not typical of the indigenous New World peoples, and so there is not much to learn in Maya. The Maya term for 'thank you' is *dyos bo'otik* (literally, 'God pays it'), which can be nominally strengthened by putting *hach* 'very' in front of it. The standard response is *mixba'al* '(it is) nothing'. If someone thanks you and you want to thank them, you can say *ma', dyos bo'otik tech* 'no, God pays it to/for you'. Coming up with anything like 'please' is a lost cause. If you can't do without it, use *por favor* with commands and requests, but remember that it constitutes a gross gringoism. The Maya are by nature a polite and thoughtful people, so they don't need to advertise when they are being polite like we do. Some commands can be softened by prefixing the word *chan* 'little' to them, for example, *pa'ten waye'* 'wait here for me' versus *chan pa'ten waye'* 'just wait here a bit for me', but the cases in which this can be used is limited to activities in which duration is an issue. When giving someone something as a gift, one pays *pa'tak tech* 'it should stay with you' to indicate that one is transfering ownership.

Another thing people want to know about is 'yes' or 'no', and while denial is easy—*ma'* 'no'—affirmation is another story, because there is no word that corresponds exactly to 'yes'. A positive response to a question is given repeating the verb or at least part of it appropriately changed for person. For example, if one asks *Uts wenech*? 'Did you sleep well?', the response is *Wenen uts.* 'I slept well.' If the question is *Taak a hanal beora*? 'Do you want to eat now?', the affirmation is *Taak.* 'Want.' There are some reasonable substitutes for these games with verb forms however. For questions dealing with something that hasn't happened yet, you can reply with *he'le'*, which really means something like 'that's the way it will be' but usually cooks down more or less to 'yes'. Another particularly useful and frequently used word is *beyo'* 'that way' which is also an affirmation but can be used with body language to mean a whole raft of things or with rising intonation as a simple question. In addition, you can learn *beya'* 'this way', which you can then use to contrast two possibilities, usually with some gesturing. Some sources assert that the word for affirmation in Maya is something like *(h)aa.* This is actually a low indefinitely sustainable sound that one Maya speaker makes intermittently while another is talking or immediately thereafter to indicate that he or she is following what is being said and is nominally in agreement with it. Many English speakers do a similar sort of thing by punctuating the speech of an interlocutor with 'uh-huh'.

Finally, there is the matter of taking one's leave. There are three possibilities, all relating to the time frame in which you expect to see the person again. If you expect to be away only for a matter of hours, so that you will see the person again that day, you say *ka'ka't(e')* 'late' or, more fully, *mas ka'ka't(e')* 'later'. If you expect to see the person the next day, you say *saamal* 'tomorrow' or, more fully, *asta saamal* 'until tomorrow'. At night, when taking leave of someone you expect to see in the morning, you can say *hatskab k'iin* 'morning', or you can simply shorten it to *hatskab.* When the time frame is greater or more indefinite, then *tu heel k'iin* 'to another day' is used. *Tu heel* is always given a reduced pronunciation so that the phrase sounds like *tuwe k'iin.* Some people use the other Maya word for 'other', *u laak',* and say *tu laak' k'iin.*

The Maya tend to like to avoid the grand scene of departure. Even after you have become quite friendly, you will find that you will be asked about your departure shortly after your arrival. The question is *Ba'ax k'iin a bin*? 'What day do you go?' which you answer with a date in Spanish, e.g., *el beynte* 'the twentieth', or a period of time, e.g., *oxp'el semanas* 'three weeks'. Likewise, as your departure approaches, you may be asked when you will be back: *Ba'ax k'iin a suut*? 'When will you return?' Try to answer honestly. It is better to express uncertainty than to say a time that you probably will not make. The Maya don't like the grand empty gesture like gringos and Mexicans. When the actual moment of your departure comes, many of your friends may have disappeared to do what they do instead of waiting around for you to leave. Do not take affront; just say a brief good-bye to anyone actually there when you leave and take off. Arrivals among acquaintances after a period of absence are friendly (and often done in Spanish by bilinguals) but tend to be understated by both gringo and Mexican standards. Em and I like to think of the Mayan world as a bit like Brigadoon, something that you just step in and out of.

There *are* some expressions to say to departing friends, which you may use when someone leaves you. Alternatively, you may befriend a somewhat Mexicanized Maya who has acquired a taste for big flashy departures with *abrazos* and corresponding expressions. The expressions are based on the construction *xi'ik tech* (plural *xi'ik te'ex*) 'may it go to you', e.g., *xi'ik tech ya'ab uts, xi'ik tech hats'utsil, xi'ik tech utsil*, etc. They all are generally equivalent to Spanish *que le vaya bien* or *buena suerte*. You should respond to any such expressions with *bey xan tech* 'likewise, you too'.

Names

When you want to introduce yourself, use only your first name or, even better, a Hispanicized version of it, Pablo for Paul, Roberto for Bob, etc. Avoid your last name, particularly if you don't have a Hispanic one. They won't remember it, and it will simply elude them. This is a good rule for getting to know "real people" in general in Mexico. Take your name and fit it into the following formula: *in k'aaba'(e)'*———. Suppose your name is Wayne. There is no Spanish equivalent, but it sounds like Juan, especially to a Mexican. In Maya the spelling would be *Hwan*, and so you would say *in k'aaba'e' Hwan*, much like Spanish *me llamo Juan*. Alternatively, you can say your name first and then follow with the *in k'aaba'*, and the result would be *Hwan in k'aaba'*. You could inquire about the new acquaintance's name by asking *Ba'ax a k'aaba'*? 'What's your name?' The person will probably just say his or her first name. Many Maya have rather baroque Hispanicized classical or Old Testament names, so you have to pay attention, although there are plenty with the usual common Mexican names. Many Maya have Maya family names, often even two put together representing paternal and maternal lineages, but there are also Maya with Hispanic family names. So a name doesn't tell you whether or not a person is Maya, except that a Maya family name like Itzá, Poot, Dzul, etc., means that a person is of Maya ancestry but may or may not speak Maya. Geography and lifestyle are better indicators of the probability of being bilingual, Maya dominant, or even a Maya monolingual.

First names are used almost exclusively in addressing or referring to people. Many Maya people do not like you to now their family names nor do men like you to know the names of their wives. The principle is that gratuitous information represents power, and while you need to know someone's first name to communicate with or about him, the family name is not used and someone's wife is best referred to as *a watan* 'your wife' or *yatan Hwan* 'John's wife'. Generally you will not be told if you do not ask, and even if you do ask, you may be ignored. Take someone's ignoring or failing to answer a question as a sign that he or she does not want to give you the information now and simply back off. Often you will find that the person wants to think about whether he or she wants to give you the information and will decide that it is indeed all right for you to know. In that case, the information will suddenly and unobtrusively become available to you.

Many Maya males have, in addition to their real names, a "handle" or nickname by which they are more often referred to in their community. When you ask about the name of an individual, this is the name that you will probably be given. Such names usually refer to an attribute of the individual, although the exact nature of the reference may be obscure even to members of the community. A common nickname for men with light complexions is *Ch'eel.* The term is basically the name of the Yucatecan jay, but it is also used to mean 'light-skinned' or 'fair', the equivalent of Spanish *güero.* The Spanish term is also used as a nickname for the individuals when speaking Spanish. I know one young man who is called *Urich* (Snail) in Maya and *Caracol* in Spanish. In other cases, only the Spanish is used, for example *Arañas* (Spiders, a thin, long-limbed young man) or *Paletas* (Pallets, a mason). Because they are often references to physical and other peculiarities, such names may seem to us almost indecent—for example, *Mudo* (Dumb) for a boy who is deaf or a female name prefixed with the feminine marker *x-* for a homosexual—but to the Maya they are terms of affection, although Maya women may make their disapproval of them known.

If you are male and around the Maya long enough, you may end up with such a nickname yourself. Many of my friends and others in the village where I live in Yucatan call me *Nohoch Maak* (Old

Man). I assume this is because I, like many persons of northern European extraction, had thinning gray hair in my forties. The Maya do not generally go gray until extreme old age, and it is not unusual for a Maya to have a full head of black hair at age seventy. The Maya are in awe of a herpetologist friend who catches snakes bare-handed as part of his work and call him *Chuk Kan* (Catches Snakes).

If the person is older or is someone toward whom one needs or wants to show deference, the title *don* (male) or *donya* (female) can be added to the first name only.

Food

The dietary staples of traditional Mayan people are corn (*xi'im*) and beans (*bu'ul*). The corn is eaten largely in the form of tortillas (*waah*). One of the major occupations of Maya women is to make tortillas (*pak'ach* or *pak'achtik waah*) for the family every day. The process consists of soaking the dry corn in water with lime (calcium carbonate) (*ta'an*) overnight. The softened corn (*k'u'um*) is then ground (*huch'*) into meal, which is turned into corn dough (*sakan*, in Spanish *masa*). Hand grinding has almost completely disappeared, and the corn is ground (*huch'ik k'u'um*) with a mill, usually a single gas- or electric-powered one (*u kuchil huch'* 'grinding place') serving an entire community. The traditional instruments for grinding were the metate (*ka'*), a portable flat grinding surface, and mano (*k'ab*), a cylindrical grinding stone. The whole operation is called *k'abka'*. The dough is patted by the woman into small flat cakes which are placed briefly on a hot metal griddle (*xamach*, Spanish *comal*) to cook. If not consumed immediately when they come off the griddle, they are stored in a large gourd (*homa'*) for later consumption. The beans are cooked with water into a soup or paste in which the tortillas are dipped. If you have occasion to eat with a traditional Mayan family, there are two important things to note. The first is that no silverware is used, and you should simply shovel the beans from their dish into your mouth with a tortilla. The second is that often the members of a family unit will eat serially so that each can have fresh, hot tortillas as they come off the griddle. So don't be "polite" and wait for others to be served. Mealtime is not a particularly social occasion for traditional Maya, and so they generally shovel away silently and immediately get up from the table when finished.

Another staple of the diet is corn mush (*k'eyem*, Spanish *pozole*, though not the meat and hominy soup of elsewhere), which is eaten hot in the morning. Or more precisely, from the Maya perspective *k'eyem* is *drunk* in the morning, and the general term for having breakfast (*desayunar* in Spanish) is *uk'ul*, the intransitive verb for 'drink'. Despite the fact that it is hot, it may be given to you by a woman saying *siis* 'cold', because of a folk-belief system having to do with items being inherently either *siis* 'cold' or *chokow* 'hot'. The trick is to balance intake of 'hot' and 'cold' items to maintain health. Alcoholic beverages, for example, are 'hot', and so eating mush will counterbalance an intake of spirits. The mush and the beans are traditionally served in a small gourd called *luch*. The daily beverage *sa'* (Spanish *atole*) is also a corn product, made by dissolving a small amount of corn flour in cold water and usually sweetened with a bit of honey (*kaab*). If there are chickens around, then eggs (*he'o'ob*) are also cooked and eaten regularly.

Meat (*bak'*) is eaten infrequently, not because the Maya don't like it, but game is available only when a hunter is lucky (not too often today in Yucatan because of overhunting) or on festive occasions (see Celebrations). Domestic animals are the traditional Maya family's bank account. When someone goes to town, the trip and items purchased and services paid for are taken care of by taking along an animal to sell there.

Nowadays you may see a hunter standing beside the highway trying to sell a trophy to passing motorists. The most common animal sold in this manner is the paca (*haaleb*, Spanish *tepezcuintle*), a dog-sized rodent with long hind legs. Less frequently, a peccary (*kitam* in Maya, *jabalí* in Spanish) or possibly a Yucatecan deer (*keeh*) is shot and sold in the same way. What the hunter holds up to offer to passing cars is the carcass, which has been opened down the middle and roasted immediately after killing to preserve the flesh. If you are adventurous, you can stop and bargain for the meat (see Buying Things, this chapter) and then take it to a restaurant to have it prepared. A common preparation is to mix the shredded meat with onions, cilantro, lime juice, and vinegar to produce a kind of mixture called *buuche* (*salpicón* in Spanish) to be eaten cold with *tsahbil wah* or *tsahbil oop'* (fried tortilla chips). Paca, peccary, deer, and game in general are widely regarded as delicacies in Yucatan. On the other hand, you may want to remember that by buying game you are contributing to the over-hunting that has decimated the wildlife on the peninsula.

The classic dishes of the Yucatecan kitchen were developed as food for city-dwelling people of European origin during the colonial period. Nevertheless, indigenous ingredients and native cooking techniques were used because the Maya did the preparation. These are what you are apt to encounter in restaurants in Yucatan, in addition to the usual generic Mexican dishes, and so I will describe them for you briefly with an eye toward the language and culture. The first thing to appear on the table is a spicy—as in hot—relish (*salsa picante* in Spanish) made with various ingredients such as onions, tomatoes, vinegar, and the mandatory ingredient, chopped pepper (*ik*). Various hot peppers are used in Yucatan, but the favorite is the Scotchbonnet pepper (*habanero* in Spanish), reputedly the hottest pepper in the world. Even if you are a hot pepper freak and groove on jalapeños, be careful with the *habanero*. The Maya term for hot sauce is *xni' pek'*, which means 'dog's nose', presumably because of what happens to one's nose while eating it. Be sure to use the term with a Maya waiter in a rural restaurant because they will be surprised that you know such a thing. Typically they will be amused that you do, but they may prefer to act as though they didn't hear you say it. I assure you that it is neither vulgar nor indecent to use the term. Let me hasten to assure those who are not aficionados of spicy food that Yucatecan cuisine is otherwise not particularly *paap* 'spicy, hot'. The idea is that everyone is free to adjust the food to their own taste by adding the amount of *xni' pek'* desired.

The distinctive spice of Yucatecan cooking is the annatto seed (*kiwi'* in Maya, *achiote* in Spanish). The seed grows in pods on a low bush, and the dried seeds are used in cooking. The color of the seed is a rich rusty red and it is quite enduring. The ancient Maya used it to color the plaster on their structures, and when you see bits and pieces of red plaster in protected places on the ruins, remember that the color has lasted a thousand years or more. The flavor of the annatto seed is truly distinctive and, in my opinion, tasty. Do not miss an opportunity to try something seasoned with it; even fried chicken (*tsahbil kaax*) is a new taste sensation in Yucatan because it is rubbed with annatto before cooking. Move over, Colonel Sanders!

Pit cooking is one of the oldest known cooking techniques and probably developed in the New World over 6,000 years ago. A cooking pit is called *piib* in Maya, and the Yucatecan pork roasted in the pit is called *piibil k'ek'en*, or *cochinita pibil* in Spanish. *Piibil kaax*, or *pollo pibil*, is chicken wrapped in banana leaves to preserve moisture and then baked. Another standard dish is grilled meat, usually pork, called *pok chuuk*. The root *pok* means 'roast' or 'toast', and *chuuk* is 'charcoal', and so it is what we would call 'grilled'. *Pok chuuk* is marinated or basted in an annatto-based sauce and is an excellent way to discover the delights of this tasty seasoning. Fish is also grilled with an annatto marinade or sauce and has the peculiar name *tikin xik'*, which literally means 'dry wing'. Finally, there is *papa ts'ules*, which is crumbled hard-boiled egg wrapped in a tortilla, dipped in pumpkin seed sauce, topped with a slightly spicy tomato sauce, and served at room temperature. The common-folk explanations of the name center on the notion that the second word is *ts'ul*, meaning 'white person' (see People), so that it is purported to mean something like 'food for the white man'. The scholars' version of the significance of the name is different, however. The party line here is that the name is a corruption of *pa'pak' sul*, two long-forgotten Maya words meaning 'smeared' and 'drenched' respectively, presumably referring to the pumpkin sauce on the tortilla. Etymological questions aside, *papa ts'ules* is a delicious and distinctive Yucatecan dish. Unfortunately, it is not on the menu at many restaurants. Look for it when you are in the Puuc region.

One-dish meals (*k'ool*, roughly 'gravy' or 'broth') are prepared by the Maya on festive occasions. The most famous is a black sauce made from toasted peppers with chunks of meat called *box k'ool*, or *relleno negro* in Spanish. Such a dish made from beans is *k'oobil bu'ul*.

Yucatan has a number of indigenous edible plants and some that have been introduced for which there are terms in Maya. These include the tomato (*p'aak*), avocado (*on*), banana (*ha'as*), papaya (*put*), guava (*pichi'*), and soursop (*oop*). The orange has a little-used Maya name, *pak'aal*, and the term *china* is commonly used. The common orange that grows all over the peninsula is the sour orange, which is *china pah*. For most other fruits and vegetables the Spanish name is used. Dairy products are not part of the Maya diet, and all are referred to by Spanish names. The same is true for most beverages other than *sa'* and *siis ha'* 'cold water'. There is an older term for 'beer', *cheeba*, but most people say *seerbeesah*. Honey (*kaab*) is the traditional sweetener; sugar is either *ch'uhuk* 'sweet (stuff)' or *asukaar*. Salt, a Yucatecan trade item from pre-Columbian times, is *ta'ab*. Its primary use is traditionally as a preservative for meat (*bak'*) or fish (*kay*).

The Maya terms for gustatory sensations are: *ch'uhuk* 'sweet', *pah* 'sour', *paap* 'hot, spicy', and *k'ah* 'bitter'.

Now that you have some idea about the Mayan food culture, I will give you a few phrases and formulas for talking about it.

Hach wi'hen.	I'm very hungry.
Wi'hech?	Are you hungry?
Hach uk'ahen.	I'm very thirsty.
Uk'ahech?	Are you thirsty?
Tu'ux ku kono'ol———?	Where do they sell———?
Tak a hanal beora?	Do you want to eat now?
Tak in t'abik k'aak' u ti'al in mak'antik in wo'och.	I want to make a fire to fix my dinner.
In k'aat(e)———.	I'd like some ———.
A k'aat(e)———?	Would you like (some)———?
Chen hump' iit (maas).	Just a little (more).
Ya'ab.	That's enough/too much.
Hach ki'.	Very tasty.
Chen lelo'.	That's all.
Wa kex ma'?	Anything else?
A k'aat u heel?	Do you want anything else?
Yan———behla'?	Have you got any———today?
Na'am.	There isn't any.
Taas ten (hump'el)———.	Bring me (a)———.
Hach ki' a wi'ih!	Bon appetit!

Traveling

Few traditional Maya can afford a car or truck, and so the usual methods of traveling are walking or riding a bicycle for (relatively)

A *colectivo* on a rural road (*sak beh*) near X-uilub, Yucatan. Note the bicycles of the passengers hanging on the back.

A man and horse returning with corn from the milpa near Cobá, Quintana Roo.

short distances and using public transportation (buses, which in Maya may be called *wawa,* and *colectivos,* small trucks or vans which meander over rural roads offering rides for a small fare— they often have blue license plates) or hitchhiking for longer ones. As you travel, you have an opportunity to talk to the Maya. If you have a car, you can offer people a ride. Remember, many people will fit in a relatively limited space in a car or truck, not only because the Maya are so small, but also because no one wants to see a possible ride go to waste. They are accustomed to riding that way, and so it is no problem and in fact preferable to leaving people standing when a large group is waiting for transportation. You should ask someone *Tu'ux ka bin(e'ex)?* (the optional ending is for more than one person). If you are going at least that far, you can say *Ten xan.* 'Me too.' and invite them to get in by saying *Taak a na'akal(e'ex)?* 'Do you want to get in/on?' A common answer that may surprise you is a (Spanish) number, e.g., *beynteuno,* which means the nearest kilometer marker on the highway to where the person is going. Apparently, the Maya have taken advantage of the government's generously granting names to where they live with the kilometer markings. One such place on the Cancun–Chetumal highway that eventually became large enough for official recognition as a town is officially called '102' (not 'Cientodos'!). If you're not going that far, you can say *Chen tak———kin bin.* 'I'm only going to———.' and let them decide if they want to go only that far. When you get near your traveling companions' destination, ask for exactly where they want out: *Tu'ux ka weemel(e'ex)?* 'Where do you get out?' The general answers are *te'lo'* 'there' and *te'la'/waye'* 'here'. At the end of the ride, the rider(s) will probably ask *Baahux?* 'How much is it?' because it is usually the case that people pay a small sum for a ride. You, however, are a very rich gringo since you have a vehicle, and so you say with great largess *Mixba'al.* 'Nothing.', and the Maya then tell you that God pays it *Dyos bo'otik.* (i.e., 'Thank you.'), which is, after all, true, or you may even receive a blessing like *Dyos ku kanantech.* 'May God protect you.'

If you travel as a consumer of public transportation and hitchhiking, the same principle operates in reverse, namely, you should be prepared to pay for a ride. Anybody who drives a motor vehicle speaks Spanish, and there is a chance that they may not speak Maya or want to speak Maya, so do the negotiating in Spanish.

Once you get in on a ride you may want to try your Maya, particularly on likely looking fellow passengers. Try the ever popular
Tu'ux ka bin? Another variant for making general small talk is to
ask where a person is from: *Ba'ax a kaahal?* 'What is your town?'
This constitutes a kind of group identity below the level of eth-
nicity and above the level of family. Be prepared for the same question, and answer with a large, well-known U.S. city or one of the
states that all Mexicans are aware of, such as California or Texas,
even though you may in fact live in a small city hundreds of miles
away. You may want to avoid mentioning Washington since the
name is the source of a Maya pun (*baaxal t'aan*) because it sounds
like *Box in toon.* 'My dick is black.' to the Maya. In any case,
hearing an at least nominally familiar name will make you more
real and less threatening. An alternative answer is simply Los Es-
tados Unidos, as many rural Maya are quite willing to believe that
the United States is a *kaah* 'town', albeit a very large one. If your
use of Maya piques someone's curiosity, you may be asked *Tu'ux
luk'ech?*, which literally means 'Where did you flee from?' What
the person means is not where you are coming from right now (see
below) but rather more generally something like what gringo tourists mean when they ask "Where did you start out from?" If the
person you're talking to was on the vehicle before you got on, you
can ask where he or she is coming from, *Tu'ux talech?* Do not be
overbearing about practicing your Maya and be prepared to sit for
long periods of silence.

If you are walking or driving, you may want to ask directions. If
you want to know where a path or road goes, ask *Tu'ux ku bin le
beha'/karetera?* 'Where does this road/highway go?' Remember,
the *beh* are primarily walking trails but can also be rural, local
unpaved roads (*sak beho'ob*, or *caminos blancos* in Spanish). A
hard-surface motorway is always a big deal and therefore referred
to by the Spanish *carretera*, in Maya *karetera*.

An important expression for going is *ko'ox* (the plural is
ko'one'ex) 'let's go', which invites participation in some common
motion. It may be followed by a verb of collective activity: *Ko'ox
hanal!* 'Let's (go) eat!' If used without another verb, it is usually
followed by the relatively meaningless *tuun* 'then', and so 'Let's
go (now)!' is best rendered with *Ko'ox tuun!*

When you arrive in a Maya town or settlement where you want
to visit or even possibly stay, the first thing to look for is a store.

Bicyclists near Hondzonot,
Quintana Roo.

Free enterprise being what it is in Yucatan like every place else, there may be more than one. You want the one that appears to be largest or most substantial. Go in and buy something (see Buying Things), such as a soda (*refreskoo*) and a snack. Buying a soda is particularly useful because you may not leave without paying a bottle deposit, which poor people consider undesirable because it ties up capital in useless bottles, or having the soda dumped into a plastic bag, usually with a small surcharge. The point is that you can use the time spent drinking the soda to make yourself known and to get whatever information you need. The people who run a store, particularly the largest store in any town, are likely to be influential. You will need to ingratiate yourself with them. If you want to spend the night, you will need a place to hang your hammock. *Hu' beeta'al in mansik aak'ab' te kaaha'?* 'Can I spend the night in this town?' *Tu'ux yan in sinik in k'aan?* 'Where should I hang my hammock?' *Hu' chabal in sinik in k'aan waye'?* 'Can I hang my hammock here?' Incidentally, if you don't travel with your own hammock for sleeping, there is no point in seeking private lodgings in rural Yucatan. You'll have to stay in cities which have hotels or areas which cater to tourists.

People

Deference is shown to old people by referring to them as *nohoch* 'large, great'. A woman of substantial years may be called *nohoch koolel* 'great woman', while a man is called either *nohoch maak* 'great man' or *nohoch tata* 'grandfather'. The first two are used to talk about such persons. Old people can be called *le nukuch ma-ako'obo'* 'the great people'. Otherwise, people are generally referred to by name. If the individual is not known, *senyor(a)!* is probably best to use to get someone's attention, but then use it sparingly thereafter, as it is not the Maya custom.

The terms of relation are, with the exception of the designations for siblings, almost exclusively Spanish. The now moribund intergenerational terms are *tatich* 'grandfather', *mamich* 'grandmother', *tat* 'father', *na'* 'mother'. The colloquial Spanish *papah* and *mamah* are the most common for the latter, and by analogy *nohoch papah* and *nohoch mamah* for the former. A term for 'grandmother' (*nohoch*) *chiich* is used to talk about one's grandmother but not in her presence or as a term of address, although it is not disrespectful. 'Son' and 'daughter' are completely extinct, and *iho* and *iha* are used exclusively. Referring to one's progeny in general, *paalalo'ob* 'children' is the usual term, and the possessed forms of the singular *paal* are used to refer to a son or daughter without gender reference. An elder sister is *kiik*, an elder brother is *suku'un*, younger brother or sister *iits'in*, and the youngest sibling *u t'upil a wiits'in*. A grandchild of either gender is *aabil*.

A moribund term for a distant relative (cousin, uncle, aunt) is *ch'ilankabil*, but almost everybody uses the appropriate Spanish terms for such persons. All the native terms are relational (see Chapter 4) and therefore are used either as address terms (i.e., what you call someone) or with the appropriate possessive pronouns. If they are used for general reference (e.g., the brother, a sister), then the suffix *-tsil* is added. It should also be noted that Maya lacks a common unambiguous native term for 'family', either in the nuclear sense or the broader one of 'relatives'. The closest available term is *u laak'* 'one's other'. The first interpretation of the expression *in laak'* is 'my brother', although if pressed a Maya will admit that it can also be used to refer to one's spouse. Similarly, the plural expression *in laak'o'ob* elicits *mis hermanos* 'my brothers' or 'my siblings' with admission to the additional possibility of *fami-*

lia. With the *-tsil* suffix added, *laak'* means 'relative'. The plural in *lak'tsilo'ob* is the totality of one's relatives, not just the (nuclear) family. If you mean 'family' in any sense, the expression is *pamilyah*, although it too is also used to mean 'wife'.

In addition to being individuals and members of families, people are also grouped in collections of those who identify themselves or are identified as a unit. One such group is the Maya themselves. The common term is *maya*, and the plural is *le maya-o'obo'*, although one often hears the native pluralization of the Spanish plural, *le mayaso'obo'*. In Spanish it is best to use *mayero*. *Masewal* (Spanish *mázehual*, a Mexican term of Nahuatl origin for 'traditional native person') is widely recognized by the Maya as referring to them, but it is a term that they do not generally use, the exception being some of the descendants of the nineteenth-century rebels for whom the term has the narrower meaning of their smaller subculture and religion (see this chapter, Systems of Belief). Occasionally, written sources refer to the Maya language somewhat pretentiously (and technically incorrectly) as *masewal t'aan.*

As mentioned above, the most basic group identity of the Maya is the community (*kaah*). An important question is whether this is a fixed identity, such as 'hometown' in the United States, or whether it shifts with changes in residence. The answer is, I think, strictly neither or perhaps both. Those Maya who move to a large town or city, particularly one without a Maya population identity, e.g., Cancun, and maintain ties through family to a smaller Maya community may also maintain the identity of their hometown. On the other hand, those Maya who move to another Mayan community and raise a family there usually shift their identities gradually onto the new community. This gives a certain ambiguity to the term *in kaahal*, but arguably it is not much different from the way North Americans use the expression "I'm from————." In any case, the term for persons from any town is formed by suffixing *-il* to the Maya name of the town, e.g., *Saki'il* 'from Valladolid', in Spanish *vallisolitano, Tikulil* 'from Ticul', *ticuleño*, etc. A *meridano* ('from Mérida', *Ho'* or *Tiho'* in Maya) is *Ho'il*, presumably because the *ti'* at the beginning is the preposition of location (see Chapter 4). The principle does not extend to the many other place names beginning etymologically with the same preposition (e.g., Ticul, above). As in Spanish, the form is basically an adjective that can be used with nouns to indicate the origin or style of the thing, e.g., *Motulil he'*, in Spanish *huevos motuleños*, 'Motul-style eggs' (a popular Yucatecan breakfast dish). The *-il* may also be added in a pinch to Spanish place-names only when the place has no Maya name, e.g., *San Hwanil* 'from San Juan', *juanista*. The B pronouns (see Chapter 4) may be added to all forms ending in *-il*, e.g., *Koba'ilen* 'I'm from Cobá'.

A person of European ancestry who is from the United States is a *gringo*. This term is not an insult and may be used freely to refer to such persons. The plural is either *gringos* or *gringoso'ob*. Among themselves some Maya use the term *sak boko'ob* (literally 'white odors') for gringos because of their penchant for perfume and cologne. Other persons may be classified in the same group by Maya for whom further division of the group which they see monolithically is gratuitous. Thus, Canadians and Europeans are also *gringos*, although sophisticates realize linguistic differences and distinguish *alemanes, franseses,* and *italianos*. Persons of African heritage are generally *negros* or *boxo'ob* 'blacks'. Persons from other parts of Mexico are *mehikanos* or *wacho'ob*. Use of the latter term is in decline, although most people know it, and it can also mean 'soldiers', who were the first Mexicans the Maya got to know in the nineteenth century. Etymologically, it is believed to have come from a term meaning something like 'the tall ones'.

The final set of ethnonyms have to do with non-Mayan persons who live on the Yucatan peninsula. The Spanish term *yucateco* traditionally means a person of European origin from the peninsula. It is also used officially as the designation for residents of the Mexican state of Yucatan, which is only one of three such polities on the peninsula. Residents of Campeche are officially *campechanos*, while those of the new state of Quintana Roo are cursed with the neologism *quintanarooenses*. I suspect that the probability of a traditional Maya resident of the state using such a term to refer to himself or herself and local compatriots is about the same as having a cenote ice over. In general, *mestizo* is a term used in Mexico for persons of some indigenous ancestry who identify not with their Indian heritage but rather as participants in modern Mexican society. On the peninsula, however, as I mentioned early on, it has come to acquire the purely social, nonethnic meaning of 'working-class', roughly like 'blue-collar' in the United States.

The term is not often used by the Maya in either sense, although curiously *mestiza* is a common term used to mean a woman who customarily wears the *iipil*, the native dress of traditional women. Finally, the terms *ts'ul* (for males or generically) and *xunaan* (for females) are traditionally the Maya terms for the European inhabitants of the peninsula. However, they can be and often are applied to white strangers generally. Asked to explain the term, however, most Maya define *ts'ul* socio-economically as a rich person or someone from the city. If people feel comfortable enough to call you *ts'ul* or *xunaan* to your face, then you know that you are making progress. The wife of a white man may be referred to as *u xunaan*, something like 'his lady'.

Celebrations

Each community has at least one celebration (*cha'an*) annually to which it is devoted. Often these are nominally Catholic feast days, the exception being the *ch'achaak*, or rain ceremony. Rather than describe some in detail, I will give a generic characterization and allow you to observe the specific form that things take if you have the good fortune to be invited to attend one.

The two omnipresent features of Mayan celebration are food preparation and drinking. The food preparation will involve the preparation of meat, usually by the men, and tortillas by the women. In the *ch'achaak* there is no participation by the women at all, and the men prepare special breads called *xnohwaah* 'big tortillas' as well. If both sexes are involved in the celebration, there will probably be relatively little interaction between them. Drinking is done only by the men, who are binge drinkers, which is to say that they drink only to become as intoxicated as possible. In fact, the only words for drinking are *kala'an* 'intoxicated' and *kaltal* 'become intoxicated'. The intransitive verb for 'drink' *uk'ul* is used to mean 'to have breakfast' (see this chapter, Food)! The traditional beverage, called *baalche'*, is fermented from honey (*kaab*) which is flavored with tree bark (*u sool baalche'*). The *baalche'* has largely lost out now to the convenience and potency of cheap commercial Mexican spirits, which are purchased in town. Because these are typically flavored, they are usually referred to as *aaniis*. One popular brand is sealed with a red plastic cap and is

Women making tortillas for the Feast of the Holy Cross near Manuel Antonio Ay, Quintana Roo.

Men preparing *buuche* at the Feast of the Holy Cross near Manuel Antonio Ay, Quintana Roo.

A ring for bullfights under construction at Nuevo X-can, Quintana Roo.

called *chak pol* 'red head' by the "in" crowd. No one is obliged to *kaltal*, but those who are *kala'an* are treated rather deferentially, with the women trying gently to keep them from hurting themselves. At some point before the drinking gets serious, there is usually a religious service conducted either by a shaman (*hmen*) or a Ladino Catholic priest.

Entertainment may include music and bullfighting or some imitation thereof. It is a curious fact that the Maya, who have preserved so much of the ancient economic, material, linguistic, and religious culture, have almost completely lost their music. In the twentieth century, the music and dance was first the *paax k'ool* (Spanish *jarana*), a peninsular form that originated among the whites although some Maya now identify it as "*música maya*," but now other kinds of Mexican popular music, including mariachis, rock and roll, and even Mexi-rap, are now pervasive. Naturally the terminology for this is Spanish, although the generic words 'music' (*paax*), 'song' and 'singing' (*k'ay*), and 'dancing' (*ook'ot*) are still used. In a few remote villages a more traditional kind of Mayan music called *maya paax* played on homemade instruments can still be heard. Bullfighting (*pay wakax*, literally 'incite cattle') is also a cultural borrowing, and the terminology is therefore predominantly Spanish. A small *plaza* (Maya *k'axche'*) is often constructed out of sticks just for the occasion in small communities, which have no other need for a bullring. At a small local celebration where the bullfighting is not serious but uses only young local cattle, you may be asked *Ha' pay wakxe'?*, which is your invitation to climb into the ring and give it a try.

Work

Although some modern Maya are wage earners or proprietors of small businesses, the only real occupation for a traditional Mayan man is tending a milpa (*kol*). Milpa is the Spanish term (now also used in English) for a slash-and-burn field, which is made and tended in virtually the same way it has been for two thousand years. The soil is very poor, and a milpa may be used only two or three years before it is abandoned to lie fallow for about a decade. The cycle of the milpa begins at the end of the rainy season (November–December) when the forest (*k'aax*) is cut (*ch'akik che'*) to clear space for the milpa. The low growth (*k'aax*) is cut with a machete (*yetel maskab*) and with a brush hook (*yetel xloob*), while small trees are removed with an axe (*yetel baat*). The cuttings are left to dry in the field because at the end of the dry season in May they are burned (*toka'an*) to fertilize the soil. The decision about the time to burn is crucial because if it is done too early, the cutting will not be dry (*ma' tikni'*) and the burn will not yield the nutrients necessary to make the poor soil fertile. On the other hand, if the *milpero* (*kolnaal*) waits too long, the rains (*chaak*) will come, and the burn will be impossible. After the burn and the rains come, the *milpero* goes to his field to plant (*pak'al*) with a pointed planting stick (*yetel xuul*), which he uses to make a hole into which five corn seeds (*u neek' xi'im*), a couple of beans (*bu'ul*), and a couple of squash seeds (*sikil*) are placed. Additionally a couple of lima beans (*iib*) may be added. Out of this grows a clump of cornstalks about which the bean vines climb while the squash (*k'uum*) runs about the base. Because the soil is so poor, the rain must be fairly constant to sustain the growth. A particularly crucial time requiring rain is when the young plants are

Cutting a milpa near X-uilub, Yucatan.

Burning a milpa near Cobá, Quintana Roo.

Milpa after burning near Cobá, Quintana Roo.

growing rapidly in late August and September. Many communities hold a rain ceremony (*ch'achaak*) at this time to bring (*ch'a'ik*) the rain spirits (*yunchaako'ob*). Another risk through the late part of the growing season is that of the hurricanes and violent storms (*chak iik'al* or *chich iik'* 'strong wind') that come from the east off the Caribbean Sea and can ruin the corn and beans. After the corn is grown, the ears (*nalo'ob*) are usually bent down (*wats'a'an*) by the *milpero*.

The *milpero* harvests the crops by hand into a cone-shaped basket (*xuux*) which he wears on his back. He measures his fields in *mecates*, a unit of area twenty meters by twenty meters. The Maya word for *mecate* is *p'isik'aan* 'measure'.

If you want to visit a milpa, do so only in the company of its tenant. There are two reasons for this. First, although a milpa is a sacred place where the farmer works very hard and feels secure, it is also quite dangerous. The greatest danger is snakes (*kano'ob*), and the most dangerous is the fer-de-lance viper (*kwatro naris[es]*,

Harvesting corn in a milpa near Manuel Antonio Ay, Quintana Roo.

literally 'four noses' for its distinctive marking), which is very aggressive and whose bite can kill in twenty minutes. The other reason is that the farmer has enlisted the help of forest spirits (*aluxes* in Spanish; Maya *aluxo'ob* or *k'ato'ob*) by bringing them a gourd of gruel (*u luch saka'*) to show them that he loves them. In return the *aluxes* stand guard over the milpa to chase away birds and strangers like you when the farmer is away.

You may want to learn the following phrases about the milpa.

Taak in ximbal ich kol.	I want to visit a milpa.
Hu' beeta'al a we'esik ten a kole'?	Can you show me your milpa?
Yan kano'ob te'lo'.	There are snakes there.
Hayp'el p'isik'aan yan tech ich kol?	How many *mecates* do you have?
Ba'ax k'in a tookik a kol?	When will you burn the field?
Ba'ax k'in a pak'al?	When will you plant?

Carrying thatch palm with a tump
line near Cobá, Quintana Roo.

Domestic Life

The traditional Mayan household is centered on a small piece of
land within a community. Various Spanish terms are used to indicate the size and organizational type of community. The smallest
is a *campamento* 'camp', which is a couple of families living together and using a common water source but with no real government recognition and services. The *ejido*, a collective, has been
the form of rural organization promoted by the Mexican government. In Maya all communities, small and large, are called *kah*
'town'. In any case, the land on which the family lives, called a
solaar, often is surrounded by a wall (*pak'*). The main structure is
the house (*nah*). The classical form for the *nah* is apsidal, a rect-
angle with circular ends. Many are now simply rectangular. The
construction is traditionally exclusively from materials extracted
from the forest. The foundation and floor are made of broken
pieces of limestone covered with dirt which is pressed and
smoothed. The four pillars (*okom*) inside support the structure.
The roof (*u pol nah*) is sharply pitched and covered with palm
thatch (*xa'an*). The walls are covered with small vertical sticks

Repairing a roof in Macario Gomez, Quintana Roo.

(*kolo'ohche'o'ob* or *chuuyche'*). Commercial building materials
are introduced in varying degrees according to the taste and pock-
etbook of the owner/builder. Usually a cement floor is favored if
possible. Walls made from cement and either concrete blocks or
native stone produce a *pak'il nah* 'walled house'. Corrugated
metal or composition roofing is also used, or a *pak'il nah* may be
given a flat concrete roof in the Mexican style. At one end is the
kitchen (*k'ooben*), really just the cooking fire and food preparation
materials that the woman of the house uses. The fire (*k'aak'*) is
bordered by three large stones (*oxp'el tuunich*) which support the
griddle (*xamach*) while making tortillas or pots when boiling water or cooking. The hammock (*k'aan*) is the place not only for
sleeping but also for resting or lounging during the day. If there are
many people living in the house, hammocks may be removed during the day but one or two are left for lounging. Half pieces of logs
called *k'aanche'* (literally 'wood hammocks') are used for sitting,
especially while cooking. The description here is traditional and
may be broken by many modern intrusions including a table,

A house in Chan Chen, Quintana Roo.

chairs, bottled-gas cooking stove, electricity, lighting, refrigerator, radio, and television. One eminent North American linguist has referred to the last item as "cultural nerve gas."

Outside the house in the yard are the domestic animals, such as chickens (*kaax*), turkeys (*uulum*), and pigs (*k'eek'en*), which constitute the family's access to cash. The omnipresent feature outside the house is the raised garden (*ka'anche'* literally 'sky wood') for raising herbs and small plants. It has stick legs that keep the plants one to one-and-a-half meters off the ground. On top, a hollow log is used to hold the soil and plants. More modern versions have a flat top with buckets and large cans used to hold the plants. Also in the yard there may be banana plants (*ha'as*), orange trees, and other fruit plants for consumption by the family or sale to make a little money. Finally, there is a trough, traditionally hewn out of a log but now often commercially produced from plastic or other material, in which clothing and other items are washed (*p'o'a'al*). The trough is known only by the Spanish name *batea*.

A raised-bed garden (ka'anche') near
Manuel Antonio Ay, Quintana Roo.

If you want to go to someone's house, stop at the perimeter of
the yard and yell out something like *ola!* to get someone's attention if no one sees you coming. If you are a stranger, you will
need to ask permission to approach the house: *Hu' chabal in naats'kimbae'¿* 'May I approach?' A nod or gesture will then allow
you to advance.

Once you reach the person meeting you, greet him (or her) and
state your business. If you are looking for someone or something,
you may use *Tin kaaxtik (hump'el)———.* 'I'm looking for (a)
———.' Or you may want to learn the location of something *Tu'ux
yan———¿* 'Where is———?'

Buying Things

I have refrained from using the word 'shopping' here because there
are really only two places that you can use Maya to make purchases. One is in the small stores that one finds in rural areas; the
other is with street vendors.

The way purchases are made in rural stores is as follows. The customer steps meekly to the counter and states in a low voice with as few words as possible (usually one) the category of things he or she wishes to purchase. The clerk may then ask for further details of the purchase, e.g., *Hayp'el?* 'How many?' or *Baahux?* 'How much?' If the clerk has reason to doubt whether the customer has the wherewithal to make such a purchase, he will say *Tohol?* 'Price?' meaning the customer should show him the money before he goes to the trouble of getting the merchandise. This lack of faith in the customer's means is unlikely when the clerk is confronted by a gringo, but you should be aware of the routine.

When the purchase is placed on the counter, the customer asks *Baahux?* and the clerk replies with a number in Spanish, typically with the *mil* 'thousand' for the number of pesos left off. A currency reform instigated by the Mexican government at the beginning of 1993 introduced the *tumben peso* 'new peso' which is the equal of one thousand *uchben pesos* 'old pesos', which renders transactions in thousands of pesos unheard of in the daily life of rural Mexico. Not surprisingly now, this change seems to have the opposite effect and has given new life to talking about pesos in terms of *mil.*

The customer will then ask about the next item which he or she wishes to purchase. And the same routine follows, minus the inspection of means because the customer has already established assets during the first purchase. The practice is to pay for each item in turn, thereby saving both the customer and the clerk the problems of complex mathematics associated with totaling up a bill at the end. The clerk may wish to show you his worldliness by totaling up all your purchases to pay for at once, just like in the big city. In that case, he will ask *Chen lelo'?* 'Is that all?' or *Wa ba'ax mas?* or *Ba'ax u heel?* 'Something else?'

With street vendors and in markets the opportunities to use Maya are somewhat more circumscribed. They are used to selling primarily to *ts'ulo'ob,* using Spanish to do it, of course. For market items, the price is established by the competition, and generally there is no bargaining. You can ask the price *Baahux (u tohol)* ———? 'How much is (the price of)———?' and then ask for a certain amount, *Ts'a ten*———. 'Give me———.') Amounts and prices have to be done in Spanish, except for those items counted individually between one and four, with -*p'el* (inanimates) or -*ts'it* (long things) or -*tul* (in case you are in the mood to buy a live animal). If you want to try bargaining on handcrafts, hammocks, etc., in Maya, ask the price and then with appropriate contemplation and examination of the merchandise respond *hach ko'oh* 'too expensive'. I am a crummy bargainer because I loathe doing it. If the technique interests you in general, read the appropriate sections (chapters 12 and 23) in Carl Franz's *The People's Guide to Mexico* (see Chapter 7).

Flora and Fauna

The degree to which the Maya know the names for plants and animals varies widely among individuals, just as it does among English speakers. As you know from our own society, intensive and accurate knowledge of names and classifications of flora or fauna is esoteric, that is to say, something that distinguishes one as a specialist, usually by dint of some kind of formal or informal training in the area.

Since detailed treatment is beyond the scope of this general introduction to modern Maya language and culture, I am going to treat the field largely by giving you a few references to the technical literature, particularly for those areas of specialized interest, which may be of assistance. Otherwise, of course, if you are a botanist, ornithologist, herpetologist, or whatever, you would be well advised to keep your own lists and seek out native specialists who can help you find and classify whatever interests you. Do not depend completely on the accuracy of the literature because there is inevitably local variation for designations as well as changes that take place over time.

General knowledge of fauna extends principally to large animals and categories of smaller animals. The first thing to note is that the most basic classification is the distinction between domestic animals (*aalak'o'ob*) and animals of the bush (*ba'alche'o'ob*, literally 'tree things'). The glossary gives the general terms for many of the commonly seen animals of both categories. As wildlife disappears from the forests of the Yucatan, the Maya names for it also tend to disappear and Spanish designations are used.

Conversely, as new forms of domestic animals are introduced, they are called only by a Spanish name, e.g., *pato* 'duck'.

With snakes, the popular Spanish designations are used to identify types. The most feared and discussed viper, the fer-de-lance, or *nauyaca*, is known only by the Mayanized Spanish descriptive name *kwatro naris*. Only the rattlesnake is known sometimes as *tsab kan*, which is descriptive just like the English and Spanish (*serpiente de cascabel*), but the popular term is the Spanish term shortened to *cascabel*. The standard survey of the snakes of the peninsula is K. P. Schmidt and E. W. Andrews, "Notes on Snakes from Yucatan" (Zoological Series, Field Museum of Natural History 20 [1936]: 167–187), supplemented by E. W. Andrews, "Notes on Snakes from the Yucatan Peninsula" (Zoological Series, Field Museum of Natural History 20 [1937]: 355–359). Schmidt and Andrews give the Maya designations for snakes as these were available to them.

The entire peninsula is a birder's paradise, and even for the casual observer the birds' variety and beauty are an unending source of delight while driving or walking in rural areas. Raymond A. Paynter, Jr.'s, great study of the birds and their distribution, *The Ornithogeography of the Yucatan Peninsula*, (New Haven: Peabody Museum of Natural History, 9, 1955) contains the Maya names for a surprisingly large number of birds in a precise and consistent transcription.

For flora, there is the monumental study by Ralph Roys, *The Ethno-Botany of the Maya* (Philadelphia: Institute for the Study of Human Issues, 1976), which was based on very different field conditions sixty years ago. There are still shamans (Maya *hmeno'ob*, Spanish *curanderos, yerbateros*) who practice traditional use of botanic remedies. Those interested in botany would do well to seek out such persons as consultants.

The following phrases may be helpful in your nature study.

Tin kaaxtik———u ti'al in meetik pootoos.	I'm looking for ———to photograph.
Yan (———) waye'?	Are there any (———) around here?
Tu'ux ku yila'al (———)?	Where can you see them/ (———)?
Ba'ax u k'aaba' lelo'?	What is that called?

| *Yan u k'aaba' ti' Maya t'aan xan!* | Does it have a Mayan name also? |
| *Kanantaba(e'ex)!* | Watch out! Be careful! |

Systems of Belief

If the old adage that there are no atheists in foxholes is true, then the same holds for milpas. The traditional Maya are strongly spiritual people who accept that the world is strongly influenced by unseen powers with which they must work in harmony on an ongoing basis. The organization of faith among the Maya falls into three groups. The largest and oldest group is those Maya who accept the Roman Catholic Church as it exists in Mexico and therefore refer to themselves as *católicos*. The practice of those Maya who live in the cities and towns of the peninsula is centered on the churches available to them in those communities. The priests, who are almost exclusively non-Maya, often serve a number of such communities. To fill the gap left by the absence of Maya priests in colonial times, the institution of native lay leaders, usually called *maestros cantores*, developed. They are available to lead various kinds of rituals short of a mass. The most frequent is the novena. In the twentieth century women have taken a role as lay leaders in such services, and they are called *rezadoras.* The most important qualification for such leadership is being literate both in Maya and Spanish. Although printed materials, particularly in Spanish, are sometimes available and in the possession of lay leaders, most also keep their own handwritten books in which to record various songs and rituals for use in leading services.

A strongly Maya variation of the Catholic cross is one without the figure of Jesus on it but instead dressed in an *iipil.* Such crosses are called *santos* and are characteristic of the eastern part of the peninsula, particularly in the Maya Church (see below).

The Maya of the forest and remote villages have little direct access to the Church except for their infrequent visits to town or, even more infrequent, visits by a priest to their communities. Particularly here, what is called "Catholic" becomes strongly syncretized with traditional beliefs in the *yuntsilo'ob,* the forest spirits, which include the rain spirits (*yunchaako'ob*) and guardians of milpa (*aluxo'ob*) mentioned earlier. A third category is the *baal-*

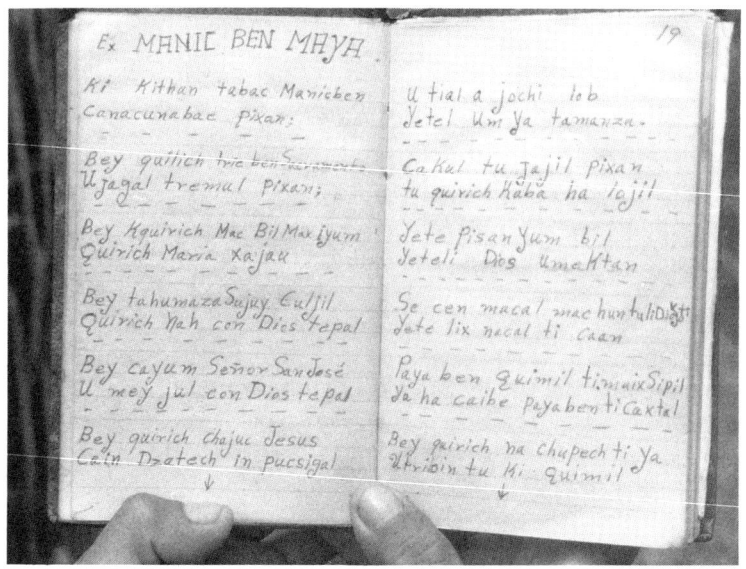

A Maya religious tract in the chapbook of a *maestro cantor* in Tikuch, Yucatan.

mo'ob, who are the guardians of the forest. There is also a category of malevolent beings called *xtabayo'ob*. A *xtabay* is a ghost or evil demon that takes the form of a beautiful woman who lives in the trunk of a ceiba tree (*u chun ya'axche'*) and goes after men passing through the forest alone to seduce them, with fatal consequences. The esoteric knowledge of putting traditional beliefs and knowledge of herbal medicines to use is the province of the *hmen*, the Maya shaman.

During the Caste War in the nineteenth century, the Maya rebels who occupied and held the forests of the eastern part of the peninsula were cut off from the European Catholicism and developed their own form of it which is based on their earlier experience with the colonial Catholicism and their long rebellion against the white power structure of Yucatan and Mexico. The term *iglesia masewal* 'Maya Church' is now sometimes used as an appellation for this religion. There are at least four places, all in Quintana Roo, where there are still Maya Churches, and these Maya have been the object of considerable interest by anthropologists in this century.

Mayan crosses on an altar near
Manuel Antonio Ay, Quintana
Roo.

The final religious institution which has a following among the
Maya is a range of North American evangelical Protestant groups,
which are generally referred to as *evangélicos*. They are the product of aggressive missionization that funnels down from the North
through Mexican branches of these churches. *Evangélicos* tend to
attract those Maya for whom the modern world has a strong ap-
peal because they strongly reject not only Catholicism but also
traditional beliefs and practices such as the rain ceremony and
shamanism. The evangelical movement has permitted the tensions which exist in the small homogeneous Maya communities
to polarize around the issue of religion, and you should be aware
that the antipathy of each group for the other is, unfortunately,
very real.

Your interest in the Maya and their religion will generally be
accepted if you show appropriate respect for their sensibilities.
First, you should dress with appropriate modesty. Women should
note the amount of anatomical exposure of the *iipil*, the native
woman's dress, and try to generally emulate that. Avoid the temp-
tation in the hot climate to wear things like short shorts, halter
bras, or anything with a bare midriff when you will be with the

A Mayan Catholic Church in Hondzonot, Quintana Roo.

Maya. On the other hand, "going native" by donning an *iipil,*
which can easily be purchased in some gift shops and from street
vendors, is likewise probably ill-advised. Women implicitly show
their support of Maya traditional values to some extent by wearing
the *iipil,* and a gringa in one may be offensive to the sensibilities
of older women, particularly if she engages in "un-Maya-like" be-
havior such as chatting socially with men, driving a car, drinking
alcohol, smoking, and so forth. They are very beautiful, and if you
buy one, simply save it to wear when you get home.

Be prepared to remove your shoes when entering a church or a
shrine, although not all places expect this. Photographs should be
taken only after specific permission to do so has been obtained:
Hu' chabal in meetik hump'el pootoo waye'/teche'/te'exe'? 'May
I take a picture here/of you/of you all?' This is a good rule to follow in general when taking pictures of people and their personal
property, as well as of religious shrines. People whose pictures are
taken are best compensated by giving them copies, if possible: *Hin
taasik teche' ti'*———. 'I'll bring them to you in———.' Once

one's reputation as a gringo who is generous with photos is established in a community, one is frequently asked to take pictures, as
few traditional Maya can afford the luxury of a camera or would
be inclined to want to deal with its complexities. If returning photos is not a realistic possibility, then some small monetary com-
pensation may be in order. In fact, you may be presented with a
price when you ask. A typical innocuous way for them to do this
is to respond to your request to take a photo with the question:
Yan hump'el Koka? 'Is there a Coke?' meaning 'Will you give me
the price of a *refreskoo?*' The response is simply *Yan.*, and then
you give them the going price at a rural store. You may be asked for
a more substantial amount, however. If you would rather bring a
copy, say *Ma', min bo'otik, pero hin taasik/tuuxtik tech ti'*———.
'No, I'm not going to pay, but I'll bring/send it to you in———.'
Remember, however, that most traditional Maya have no mail de-
livery, as the Mexican postal system generally has no rural deliv-
ery on the peninsula.

   If you have occasion to visit a Maya Church (i.e., the descen-
dants of the rebels), you need to be especially sensitive to their
desire for secrecy and respect for the mystery of their religion.
These churches are always securely locked so that you may enter
only with a local personage to show you. Permission to enter may
be difficult or impossible to obtain. You have to be willing to accept the possibility that you simply will not get in. Give up gracefully. There you must remove your shoes and you may *not* take
photographs or make recordings. Likewise, you should not approach the *gloria,* or altar space, where the sacred crosses are kept.
You will have to kneel and genuflect at appropriate times during a
service.

   Religious terminology is almost exclusively borrowed from
Spanish (or Latin) nowadays in Maya.

Games and Play

The Maya, like most people, engage in structured leisure activities, but games are almost exclusively a male activity. Even young
girls who are old enough to understand the structure of, say, a
board game will eschew an opportunity to play, presumably be-

cause they have enough of a sense of gender roles to want to avoid such things.

In remote areas, it is a real pleasure to watch the spontaneity and creativity of Maya children's play. As the "modern" world encroaches, however, television and commercial toys (e.g., toy guns, plastic Ninja Turtles, etc.) replace such play. The ultimate attraction (and poison) is video games, which spread like a blight through Maya communities and become a virtual addiction for pre-adolescent boys.

The favored adult game is dominos (*dominoo*). It is played very simply, running two ways off the starting double to see who goes out first. The Maya keep count of the number of each number out on the board, and if you do not do the same, you will lose every time. Dominos are an excellent way to pass time with the Maya while you are learning their language because it takes the focus away from your fumbling around in the language. You should carry a set of double-sixes with you, and you can then invite an acquaintance to play: *Taak a baaxal* (*dominoo*)? 'Do you want to play (dominos)?' The counting is usually done in Spanish, but your pedantry will probably be admired if you insist on doing 'one' through 'four' in Maya. A double is *mula*, presumably from *mul* meaning 'together'. For indicating that it is your opponent's turn, you simply add: *Tech*. If you're skunked (you can't play with the dominos you are holding), you say: *Mina'an tu'ux*. Or, if your opponent hesitates, you can say the same thing with rising intonation as a question. The answer is either *Yan.* meaning 'I can play.' or *Mina'an.* (or its variant *Na'am.*) meaning 'I can't play.' For going to the bone pile (no name in either Maya or Spanish that I can find), you say *Yan in kaaxtik.* 'I've got to look (for it).' To tell your opponent to do the same, you say *Kaaxte!* 'Win' and 'lose' are the Spanish words *ganar* and *perder*, which take the suffix *-nah* to form the completive. 'John won.' is *Ganarnah Hwan.* and 'I lost.' is *Perdernahen.*

After people get to know you, you can be a bit more imaginative about games. My wife, for example, takes a Spanish-language Scrabble set and plays bilingual Spanish-Maya Scrabble with the young men. To make the Maya work in Scrabble you have to use a Colonial spelling system (both *c*s and *k*s for plain and glottalized velar stops, *dz*, *pp*, and *cch* for the other glottalized consonants—

see Pronunciation and Spelling) and ignore the glottalization of vowels.

The Maya also enjoy sports. Like most Mexicans, they watch spectator sports on television, if one is available. Almost every village has a basketball or volleyball court where the young men gather in the late afternoon and play until dusk. My experience is that generally gringos are not welcome to join in, presumably because a gringo of even average height must look like Shaquille O'Neal to the Maya. Baseball is the team sport about which the Maya are absolutely passionate, however. Even small, remote villages have teams made up of their young men, and on Sundays in the middle of the day under the blazing tropical sun the honor of the most humble village is defended in fierce but friendly competition against neighboring villages. Linguistically the games are quite interesting because the Spanish baseball terminology is a mix of English with calques in Spanish. The Maya have themselves developed a limited number of native baseball terms (e.g., *p'uch* as an intransitive means 'to bat', cf. *p'uchik* 'hit with a stick', and *chiin* 'to pitch', cf. *chiinik* 'throw stones at'), and so the air is alive with expressions shouted in three languages, including plenty of razzing and profanity in Spanish. Stop by to watch one if you have an opportunity.

Time

Concepts of time in modern Maya have been heavily influenced, if not overwhelmed, by Spanish, although time was an object of intense interest and classification by the Maya in both the pre-Columbian and colonial periods. In this sense it has suffered the same fate as the native numeration (see Chapter 4) to which it is, of course, closely related.

In talking about time it is useful to distinguish between relative time and fixed time. By relative I mean expressions whose meaning is determined by the context in which they are used. The most obvious examples are expressions like 'today' and 'yesterday', which are sometimes called "shifters." These survive in Maya in expressions like *behla'* 'today', *ho'lyak* 'yesterday', *saamal* 'tomorrow', and *ka'beh* 'the day after tomorrow'. One unusual Maya time concept is *oxbeh* 'the day after the day after tomorrow'. Look for an opportunity to use it. Logic would dictate that there should be an expression *kambeh for 'four days from today', but as far as I can tell, it doesn't exist, probably because use of Maya forms of 'four', e.g., *kamp'el, kantul,* etc., is on the wane. The expression for 'now' *beora* is a Maya-Spanish hybrid, as is the related term *beorita* 'right away, just now', corresponding to Spanish *ahorita.* General past time is expressed by the terms *uuchil(ak)* and *ka'chi* 'earlier, previously'. The latter is used at the end of sentences to express the content of the sentence in past time. It appears frequently in Latin- or Spanish-based grammars of Maya to give expressions such as the pluperfect ('I had seen it') and past progressive ('I was seeing it') that are grammaticalized in European languages but not in Maya. *Uuchilak* is a topic and is often used in the highlighted verbal position to emphasize that one is talking about the way things used to be. Many of the auxiliaries used with the incompletive aspect (e.g., *yan, tan,* etc., see Chapter 4) require or invite a future temporal interpretation. The term *wal(e')* 'perhaps' is used very much like *ka'chi* to give or strengthen a future temporal meaning.

General repetitive time is expressed by *sansamal,* which is *saamal* 'tomorrow' with its root reduplicated (*saam* + *saamal* 'tomorrow, tomorrow'). It is usually translated 'every day' but can be generalized to 'over and over, regularly'.

The only real surviving native unit of absolute time is *k'iin,* with a literal meaning of 'sun' but used to mean 'day'. The temporal interrogative *bik'ix* 'when' is understood but largely abandoned in favor of expressions like *ba'ax k'iin* 'what day', *ba'ax ora* 'what time (specifically)', and *ba'ax tyempo* 'what time (generally)'. With *kada* 'each, every' only Spanish time expressions are used, even *kada dyae* 'every day'. *Ha'ab,* the old Maya word for '(solar) year', is generally understood especially by the older generation but little used even by them, mostly in *u ha'abil* 'his/her age'. The use of *anyo* is pervasive. For calendrical time Spanish terms are used exclusively, but the Maya suffix -*ak* is regularly added to the days of the week to mean the previous one, e.g., *sabadoak* 'last Saturday'. The suffix can also be added to *behla'* as *behla'ak* to mean 'earlier today' or *anyo* as *anyoak* to mean 'last year'. 'Next year' is *tu heel anyo.*

For everything else relating to time, Spanish is used.

Language

In learning a language as an adult, it is often necessary to use meta-linguistic discourse. In order to go with the flow of using the language, you should try to do as much of the meta-linguistic discourse as possible in Maya. The simplest thing to do is find out what things are called. For this you can point and say *Ba'ax u k'aaba'?* or *Biix u k'aaba'?* 'What's it called?' If the object is not available to be pointed to, you can add the Spanish name after the above expression. You may get a puzzled look because the person you're asking is uncertain or doesn't know. In that case you may ask *A wohel?* 'Do you know?' The negative answer is *Min wohli'.* 'I don't know.', which is a very useful expression for you, in any case. Sometimes if you point and ask for the name, you will get the Spanish name. In that case, it is useful to make sure that there is no Maya term, at least not one that the person knows. So you then ask *Mina'an t'aan ich Maya?* 'Isn't there any Maya expression?' The response will be either *Mina'an.* (sometimes shortened to *na'am*) 'There isn't any.' or *Yan.* 'There is.'

It is important to keep in mind that talking about language is an unfamiliar activity for ordinary Maya, just as it is for most people, and it can therefore make them uncomfortable at first to be asked to help you in this way. It is also important *how* you approach people in doing it. This is one of the reasons that I introduced the technical term "meta-linguistic discourse" above. Unless you have some formal training in linguistics, you cringed when I used it, even though it should be fairly obvious what it means. In this paragraph I used an equivalent term, "talking about language," and my guess is that you didn't give it a thought.

When you ask Mayas to help you with their language, try to imagine how it is from their perspective. First, even if they have had a few years of formal education, concepts like "noun," "verb," "subject," "object," etc., are as unfamiliar and threatening to them in Spanish (they don't exist in Maya) as "meta-linguistic discourse" is for you. Second, even though they may be fluent bilinguals, they are not used to relating Maya to Spanish. It is an unfamiliar activity for most even to translate Spanish into Maya or vice versa, because their world is compartmentalized in ways that make it unnecessary. Third, keep in mind that such intellectual activity is work, and people who are used to chopping jungle in a

milpa for ten hours a day may find doing this kind of thing frus-
trating and tiring. You should pay people with whom you work on
the language intensively and systematically, but do it discreetly
(the best way is to shake hands with cash to transfer in your hand)
and don't overpay them. If you learn a couple of words from a
waiter or a guide at an archeological site, leave an especially generous tip. Finally, remember that some people make better linguistic consultants than others. Don't pester people for whom this
kind of thing is onerous.

For learning words other than the names for objects—verbs, for
example—the best way is to ask to have a brief chunk of Spanish
translated into Maya. Remember that asking about verbs by using
the citation form in Spanish, the infinitive, is risky and confusing
because Maya doesn't have infinitives like Spanish. Instead, ask
how to say something real and familiar in the form of a sentence
or a phrase. The way you do this in Maya is to say *Biix u ya'ala'al*
(*ich maya*)————? 'How is————said (in Maya)?' It is a good idea
to test out in actual conversation any expression that you learn to
see whether it works as you think it should. Also, the act of looking for the opportunity and then actually using the expression will
tend to fix it in your mind.

One problem is that the Maya tend to undercorrect gringos who
are learning Maya because they are, of course, flattered by your
interest but also because the culture is a very accepting one. Furthermore, since they often don't think that they themselves speak
"good Maya" (i.e., *maya puro*), they don't differentiate among variants. Take having your Maya corrected for flattery, because the
person obviously thinks that your Maya is good enough to merit
help. For you, of course, the first matter is making yourself intelligible, but eventually you may want to know whether some expression is "correct." You can ask if a phrase or sentence can be
said a certain way with the following expression: *Hu beeta'al u
ya'la'al* (*ich maya*)————? 'Can————be said (in Maya)?' Often it
is more effective, however, if you offer two possible ways of saying
something in Maya for comparison: *Makalmak t'aanil mas uts
————wa————?* 'Which expression is better————or————?' It
may be that they are equivalent. The expression for this is *Laylie.*
'It is the same.'

The final point of meta-linguistic discourse is talking about the
meaning of expressions in Maya. If you understand something of

what someone is saying, it is probably best to tough it out rather than interrupting the flow of the conversation. You should feel free, however, to ask someone to speak more slowly for you. Here you can say *T'aanen chaambeel.* 'Speak slowly.' Once you have made the point that they need to speak slowly, you can remind them while they are speaking by interjecting *Chaambeeli'.* 'Slowly.' into a pause in their speech. If you want someone to repeat what was just said, you can say *Biixi'?*, which is like ¿*Cómo?* in Spanish. If you are completely at a loss, then confess *Min na'atik.* 'I don't understand it.' The most convenient way to deal with this is to have the Maya translated into Spanish, if possible. There may be inexact translations or subtleties that are lost in translation, but all things considered, translation is probably the best way to find out what something means, at least until you become fluent enough in Maya to understand paraphrases. The expression for 'mean, signify' in Maya is *k'aat u ya'al,* a calque of the Spanish *querer decir,* literally 'want to say'. For example, *Ba'ax u k'aat u ya'al le t'aano'?* 'What does that expression mean?' can be used to find out about the meaning of an expression either immediately after the expression is used or sometime later by repeating the expression.

6. Some Final Thoughts

Anyone who is aware of the history of contacts between Westerners and native peoples almost anywhere in the world cannot help but be concerned about an attempt to promote such contacts, for what it shows is that often those who had the best intentions were exactly the ones who did the most damage. I realize that the existence of this book is not decisive to the continually increasing contacts between the Maya and gringos, but if it is successful, it may influence the nature and course of some of these contacts, ideally in a positive way.

There are two areas of particular concern to me personally for the potential misuse of the access to the Maya that this book may provide. One is that it may be used by traders in pre-Columbian artifacts. My experience has been that there are many poor Maya who have found artifacts during their work and travels in the jungle. Often they will hide these with the hope of being able to realize some cash from their good fortune because they are very poor and turning the items in to the authorities will gain them nothing. Corrupt officials may simply sell the items themselves. Thus, a friendly gringo, particularly one with whom they can communicate more easily than with most, becomes a target for attempting sales. I have been offered pieces on several occasions.

Fortunately, it is not only wrong but illegal both in Mexico and the United States to traffic in such items. On the other hand, things being the way they are, it would not be difficult to take a small piece home illegally, and frankly it is very tempting to own such a thing. It is therefore your responsibility to put the matter aside without offending or scaring the person or persons offering you artifacts. The Maya are quite aware that it is illegal, and so they will get you alone to make the offer. Tell them that the piece is very beautiful: *Hach hats'uts.* You cannot take it home: *Mu' chabal in bisik tin kaahal.* You need not point out the obvious, that it is illegal. If the seller persists, simply keep saying *Mu' beeta'al.* 'It is not done.' until he (or she) gives up.

The second potential misuse of this book is somewhat more subtle, for it is not illegal; namely, using your access to the Maya to play with their heads. By this I mean first and foremost religious proselytizing. It should be obvious from the discussion of religion above (see Chapter 5, Systems of Belief) that I consider the consequences of the evangelical push among the Maya something that came, directly or indirectly, from the North. I might also mention in the same vein at least one gringo Catholic priest who is working to bring followers of the Maya Church back under the umbrella of the Holy Father in Rome. But abuse of their gentle, accepting natures can take other forms too. My wife and I have received offers of children from people who love them very much but would be willing to give them up for adoption by us so that they could have access to the kind of educational opportunities that we would, of course, provide. My hope is that no one will use the access from this book for such purposes.

Another area of my concern is that of gifts or sales of manufactured items to the Maya. To illustrate this, I will relate a story from my early fieldwork. Some years ago I drove to Yucatan in a pickup truck with a camper, because I was to be there for several months and it gave me the flexibility to stay by myself where I wanted. While there, I worked with a man named Serapio who lived in a remote *campamento* with no services such as electricity or running water. Serapio was very patient and helpful to a gringo who was stumbling and mumbling, trying to learn his language and something of his way of life, and although I paid Serapio daily for his services, as I was leaving I wanted to do something extra for him. In my truck I had an old camp stove that used gasoline as fuel. I got the idea that having such a thing might be a considerable improvement over the smoky fire of *oxp'el tuunich,* and so I showed him how to use it and left it with him. The next year I returned to learn that the stove had been an absolute sensation for making tortillas until one day when, while Serapio had gone to gather honey in the forest, his boys playfully held lighted candles under the pressure tank on the stove. Miraculously, no one was hurt, but the conflagration consumed Serapio's house and all his family's worldly possessions. Needless to say, I felt responsible for bringing about the means for the misfortune, and since that time I have been *very* careful about what I give people. I have already mentioned money in return for services (but not gratuitously, as that leads to begging!) and copies of photographs when one returns. Clothing is another useful possibility, and while I am sure that there are others, the important thing is to think about the possible consequences, physical and otherwise, of any gift. Selling any goods you bring in from outside Mexico constitutes smuggling and is therefore illegal, so don't even think about it.

The burgeoning use of video cameras by travelers everywhere suggests that some discussion of their use with the traditional Maya is in order. Obviously, what was said earlier about photography (see Chapter 5, Systems of Belief) largely holds for videotaping, but with additional considerations. Making videotapes is really a two-edged sword. On the negative side, it is *very* invasive and threatening to anyone to be followed by some stranger pointing an ominous black box at every move one makes. As a general rule, it should be attempted only with those people whose confidence one has gained over a period of time under other, less threatening circumstances. A good way to introduce people to videotaping is at a large public event when a group of people is being deliberately put on display. Nearly ideal is a school parade (*desfile*) or contest (*concurso*). It is then crucial that the results of the taping be made available at least to key people such as community leaders, parents of children, etc. If you use a camcorder, you can play the tape through a local television, or carry your own monitor for this purpose. The best thing is eventually to make a copy of the tape for the Maya to use themselves, if a player is available. (They are very popular, and if a family has the means, they will probably have one.) In Mexico, the Sony Beta system, now moribund in the United States, is used. Often you can find an old Beta machine stored in someone's basement which you can appropriate for copying your Maya tapes. Once you can show your Maya friends what videotaping can mean for them, the prospects become enormous. For example, I recently videotaped burning a milpa in the middle of the jungle. The power of the experience of the burn is poorly represented in still photography, and the sounds associated with it are completely lost. When I showed the tape to the man whose milpa it was, his wife and another woman were there, and it occurred to me that this was probably the first time for them to experience this quintessential Mayan activity because it is done away from the family dwelling and is not women's work. The images of their lives on a screen that has in the past shown only Hollywood pap and its analogues from Mexico City create a powerful positive message to reinforce their sense of the meaning of their way of life. Nevertheless, I urge you not to head into your experience of the Maya world with a video camera plastered against your nose. Leave it at home until you have established yourself as a friend.

Ending this introduction to the Maya language and culture on such a stern note is unfortunate but necessary. With some hard work and perseverance, you can use the book while you are on the peninsula to have a really wonderful experience with a marvelous people.

Xi'ik tech utsil te'lo'!

7. Further Reading

In this section I will discuss some sources for further reading and study on the material presented in this guide.

Language Courses

The only real language course for Yucatec Maya ever developed, entitled *Spoken (Yucatec) Maya*, was done by Robert Blair and Refugio Vermont Salas in the 1960s. It was never published but is available on microfilm or hard-copy printed from microfilm from the University of Chicago Library (Photoduplication Department, 1100 East 57th Street, Chicago, Ill. 60637; the exact reference is Microfilm Collection of Manuscripts on American Indian Cultural Anthropology. Nos. 65–66. Series X). Tapes to accompany the course are available from the language laboratory of the University of Chicago. The method of the course is audio-lingual, and the Maya is written in an arcane transcription with the pitch (see Chapter 3) represented by superscripted numbers on every syllable.

The two slender volumes of *Método para el aprendizaje de la lengua maya* by Eduardo Medina Loría and Javier Gómez Navarrete (Chetumal, Q.R.: Fondo de Publicaciones y Ediciones, Gobierno de Quintana Roo, 1982) are available in the bookstores in Mérida and elsewhere on the peninsula. This course uses the direct method, pictures and charts with little or no explanation in Spanish. It looks as though it was developed for use in local adult education courses for *ts'ulo'ob* who want to learn a little Maya and suffers from extreme superficiality and a basis in *maya puro.* I expect that if you knew everything in the two volumes cold you still couldn't begin to function in Maya.

Long out of print but often available in the antiquarian bookstores in Mérida, albeit at outrageous prices, is *Compendio del
idioma maya* by Santiago Pacheco Cruz (Mérida: Imprenta "Man-
lio," 1970). "Método Pacheco Cruz," as the work is widely called,
went through seven editions from 1908 to 1970 and is a highly
iconoclastic trip through the language and other matters that
Sr. Pacheco Cruz chose to focus on, including a list of wedding
anniversaries and the usual materials associated with them copied
from an almanac. He was a member of the Maya Academy and
serves up *maya puro*, although to his credit he often lets the reader
know the status of the material he presents. It is a wonderful curiosity but not a serious help in learning the language.

Grammars

The most readily available grammar for Maya is Alfred Tozzer's
A Maya Grammar, which was written in 1921 as a technical re-
port and has been reprinted as an inexpensive paperback by Dover
(New York: 1977). Although Tozzer is one of the great figures of
Mayan archeaology and ethnography, it has never been clear to me
why Dover chose to reprint this work in their popular and valuable
series. Tozzer attempted to work within the descriptive paradigm
for indigenous languages developed by Franz Boas. The most useful section is a detailed history of Maya language studies up to
1920 and its associated bibliography.

By far the best descriptive grammar of Maya was done by Manuel Andrade with the title *A Grammar of Yucatec Maya*. It is a
study of the language from folk texts which he collected in Yucatan in the early 1930s. Andrade compiled a draft of his grammar
in 1940 shortly before his death. The draft was edited later and
made available on microfilm from the University of Chicago Library in a series related to the Blair and Salas language course
(Microfilm Collection of Manuscripts on Middle American Anthropology, No. 41). You will need to have some experience with
descriptive linguistics to use Andrade's grammar to full advantage,
but the many analyzed sentences in chapter 4, which is most of
the book, can be studied profitably in any case.

Of the Mexican grammars only the short *Gramática maya*
written by Zavala in the 1890s is readily available for purchase in

Yucatan. Like all of the Mexican grammars, it analyzes Maya as though it were Spanish or Latin. Many of the words and forms that Zavala gives do not exist in contemporary Maya. The best Mexican grammar of Maya, "La lengua maya de Yucatan" by Alfredo Barrera Vásquez, appeared in *Enciclopedia yucatanense* Vol. 6, *Yucatán actual*, pp. 205–292 (Mexico City: Edición oficial del gobierno de Yucatán, 1977, 2d ed.). It is difficult to find except in large research libraries, but it is worth looking for.

Dictionaries

The great dictionary of Maya is *El diccionario maya-español español-maya* by a team of Yucatecan scholars headed by Alfredo Barrera Vásquez under the patronage of the Mexican henequen monopoly Cordemex. The Cordemex dictionary, as it is known, appeared in 1980. It went out of print a few years later, and prices among the antiquarian booksellers in Mérida soared to over $300, about ten times the original price. It has been recently reprinted (1991) by Editorial Porrúa in Mexico City and can now be purchased for a mere $110. Despite the claim of the title page, it is not a second edition; only the references to the Cordemex company have been deleted. Such an expenditure is definitely justifiable if you have a sustained interest in the language. Also it will probably go out of print in a few years, and you will be able to carry your copy back to Mérida and sell it to pay for your trip. More seriously, there are a few things that you should know about the Cordemex before using it. It is not strictly both a Maya-Spanish and a Spanish-Maya dictionary. Rather, it is a Maya-Spanish dictionary with a Spanish index. The Maya-Spanish part was created by combining the contents of several Maya dictionaries, a substantial number of which come from the colonial period. As a result, Cordemex is really more a historical dictionary like the *Oxford English Dictionary* than an ordinary bilingual dictionary. Many of the entries and subentries have no currency at all. Particularly tempting and dangerous is the practice of trying to find out how to say something in Maya using the Spanish-Maya index. The point is that you must use the Cordemex very carefully. It is a bulky, heavy book, singularly unsuited for anything but keeping in your library at home for reference purposes.

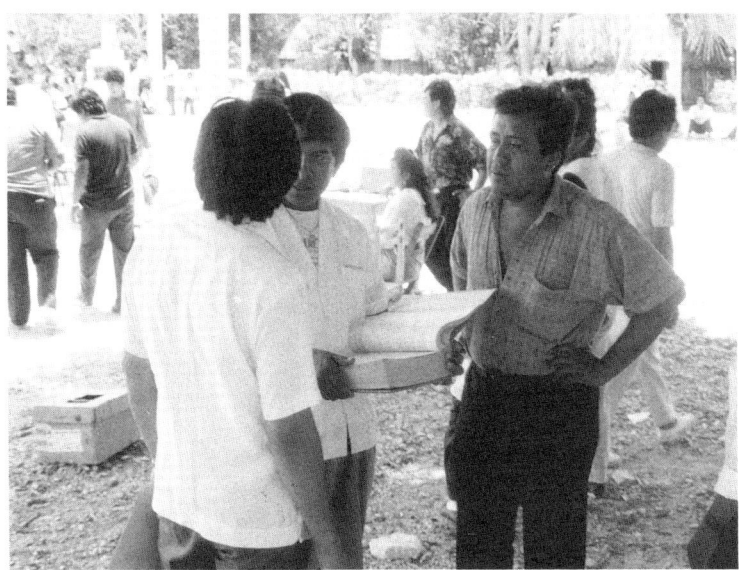

Maya teachers consulting the Cordemex dictionary at a school competition in Chan Chen, Quintana Roo.

There is also a small companion dictionary to the Zavala grammar. Many of the terms contained in it are no longer in use.

Recently, a small dictionary of modern Maya entitled *Diccionario basico Español-Maya-Español* appeared in Mérida (Biblioteca basica del Mayab, Maldonado Editores, 1992); it was compiled by Juan R. Bastarrachea, Ermilo Yah Pech, and Fidencio Briceño Chel. Its major feature is that it attempts to represent the phonemically distinct tones of the long vowels in accord with the latest (1984) "standardization" of the alphabet. The introduction features a detailed justification for this particular alphabet. Besides marking tones with accents, it differs from the alphabet used in this book (and the Cordemex dictionary) only by using *j* for *h*. The dictionary claims to represent only the vocabulary of the present day and eschews various forms and usage examples in favor of presenting lexical bases. The Spanish-Maya section gives many descriptive definitions in Maya for Spanish words that have no Maya equivalent. These may not be intelligible to ordinary speakers. It is, of course, the purest of *maya puro*, although the authors avoid

some of the standard pitfalls; for example, they simply omit
amigo from the Spanish items. The Maya-Spanish section is generally usable, however. The book is a small, slender paperback,
easily carried but so poorly made that it begins to disintegrate almost immediately. The press run was only a thousand copies, and
the supply in Mérida has practically been exhausted. Maybe gringo
demand will encourage a second and larger printing.

Texts

You may wish to improve your Maya by reading something in the
language. Bilingual collections of folktales are generally available
in the bookstores in Mérida and elsewhere and can be picked up at
nominal prices. While the texts are generally based on material
gathered in the field, they are invariably edited into *maya puro.*
Nevertheless, many useful expressions can be gleaned from these
collections. I will not make specific recommendations here because availability varies, but they are, for your purposes, all more
or less equal.

Maya Lifeways

The great studies of the folk culture of the Maya on the peninsula
were carried out as part of a large research project of the Carnegie
Foundation in the 1930s. The Carnegie project also included major
archaeological and historical studies as well. The most celebrated
ethnographic study from this period is *Chan Kom: A Mayan Village* by Robert Redfield and Alfonzo Villa Rojas, available in an
inexpensive reprint from Waveland Press (Prospect Heights, Ill.,
1989). Most of the other studies appeared only as technical reports
for the Carnegie Foundation and unfortunately may be found only
in the largest research libraries. Redfield summarized and synthe-
sized the Carnegie ethnographic studies in his 1940 book *The Folk
Culture of Yucatan* published by the University of Chicago Press
and long out of print. An expensive reprint from Gordon Press
(New York, 1976) is available, but you may be able to find the
original in a decent library that has been collecting anthropology
books since the 1940s. Redfield wrote a second book about the

village of Chan Kom after a return visit almost two decades after his initial visit. *The Village That Chose Progress: Chan Kom Revisited* (University of Chicago Press, 1950) is out of print, but it is definitely worth checking out if you can find it in a library or antiquarian bookstore, because it is really quite amusing. A more recent and engaging personal account of the Maya of Yucatan is photographer Macduff Everton's *The Modern Maya* (Albuquerque: University of New Mexico Press, 1991), richly illustrated with his stunning black-and-white photographs collected over a twenty-year period.

If you want to see what modern anthropologists do in Yucatan, you can take a look at William F. Hanks' *Referential Practice: Language and Lived Space among the Maya* (University of Chicago Press, 1990). You should be forewarned that Hanks' book is embedded in the recent thinking and jargon of such diverse disciplines as anthropology, linguistics, and analytic philosophy. If you can fight your way through (or skim over) the headier sections, you will find detailed descriptions of everyday life among the Maya in the town of Oxkutzcab in the Puuc area of Yucatan as well as excellent examples of ordinary spoken Maya.

Considerably more readable than Hanks is Paul Sullivan's recent *Unfinished Conversations: Mayas and Foreigners between Two Wars* (Berkeley and Los Angeles: University of California Press, 1991) which focuses on a historical study of the relationship between the Cruzob Maya (see Introduction) and the aforementioned anthropologists of the Carnegie Foundation in the 1920s and 1930s. The final two chapters describe the author's personal experiences with the same Maya. This work is highly recommended.

Travel

There are two classic works about eco-tourism in Mexico (although neither work uses the term): Carl Franz's *The People's Guide to Mexico* (Santa Fe, N.M.: John Muir Publications, 1992) and Bob Burleson and David H. Riskind's *Backcountry Mexico: A Traveler's Guide and Phrase Book* (Austin: University of Texas Press, 1986). The style, coverage, and approach of each is quite distinct from the other's, and yet both deal with what today we would call eco-tourism. Franz's guide first appeared in 1972, very much in the flower-child tradition of the times. Carl and his partner, Lorena Havens, have continued to update the guide on a regular basis. It is full of delightful stories about Mexico as well as solid description and advice about traveling in Mexico. *Backcountry Mexico* deals with backpacking and off-highway truck camping primarily in the arid mountainous northern Mexican states of Coahuila and Chihuahua, where both the country and the people are very different from those of the Yucatan peninsula. Extensive examples of the Spanish needed to communicate with rural people there are given. Many, but certainly not all, of the terms and phrases listed may be useful in speaking Spanish in rural Yucatan. Both books are mandatory reading for any gringo venturing into the "real" Mexico, although neither gives you any of the usual advice of travel guides about "go here, see this, eat in this restaurant, that hotel has the cleanest rooms," etc.

For this kind of information, in addition to the usual series budget-travel guides such as Fodor's, Let's Go, Real Guides, etc., there is Chicki Mallan's *Yucatan Peninsula Handbook* (Chico, Calif.: Moon Publications, 3d ed., 1992), which has the most information about places away from the usual tourist haunts. Chicki is better at helping you find a cheap hotel, a good native restaurant, or a secluded beach than she is with the fine points of archaeology and history. Her brief section on the Maya language, incidentally, is so far out of the ballpark that I don't know whether to laugh or cry.

Also dealing only with the Maya area, including Chiapas and Guatemala, is Tom Brosnahan's *La Ruta Maya* (Oakland, Calif.: Lonely Planet Publications, 1991), which trades shamelessly on the name of an ambitious project promoted by the National Geographic Society in 1989 involving the governments of the five countries of the Maya area (Mexico, Belize, Guatemala, Honduras, and El Salvador) in a regional plan for balanced economic and touristic development to protect and preserve the environmental, archaeological, and human resources of the area. Mr. Brosnahan, who established his reputation as a travel writer doing Frommer's guides and similar publications, was unable to put aside the habits of a lifetime and simply produced one more dreary "by the numbers" travel guide riddled with superficiality and inaccuracies about everything except the things that really matter to most tourists, like sleeping, eating, and shopping. Quite similar to Brosnahan's book

is the recent *The Maya Route* by Richard Harris and Stacy Ritz
(Berkeley: Ulysses Press, 1993). The latter work apparently has the
blessing of the National Geographic Society, because former editor
Bill Garrett, the "godfather" of the Ruta Maya concept, wrote the
preface, but Brosnahan beat them to the title, and so Harris and
Ritz had to settle for simply translating it into English with the
Spanish in quotation marks underneath. Yet another guide to the
peninsula and some adjacent Maya sites in Belize, Guatemala, and
Honduras is *The Yucatan: A Guide to the Land of Maya Mysteries*
by Antoinette May (San Carlos, Calif.: Wide World Publishing/
Tetra, revised ed., 1993). Although May writes in a more literate
and engaging style than the others, she still has difficulty separat-
ing fact from speculation and fantasy. Moreover, all these works
give short shrift to the modern Maya while concentrating on ruins,
colonial cities, and resorts.

Incidentally, the "Land of the Maya" map supplement to the
"La Ruta Maya" article in the October 1989 *National Geographic*
(and available for purchase from the National Geographic Society)
is a much better highway map of the peninsula than any sold locally, even though it was not so intended. The best thing is to
photocopy the part of the map you need for your travels and take
it with you in that more convenient form. There is also a Cana-
dian map, *Traveller's Reference Map of the Yucatan Peninsula*
(Vancouver: International Travel Map Productions, 3d ed., 1993–
1995), which is an attractive but inaccurate piece of overpriced
cartography. The author, Kevin Healey, apparently just sat at a
computer and scanned every map of the area he could find, never
bothering to get in a car and actually drive what he was laying out.
By far the best guide with broader coverage for all of Mexico as
well as Central America is the British book *Mexico and Central
American Handbook* edited by Ben Box (London: Trade and Travel
Publications, Ltd., annual ed.). Save the money you would spend
on a Let's Go (the Harvard students have enough money anyway)
and buy the latter book.

Glossary

This glossary contains about a thousand entries listed in a Maya-English-Spanish format and the same Maya words re-indexed in an English-Maya format. This obviously would not exhaust the vocabulary of any Maya speaker. At the same time, there may be a word or two listed here that may not be familiar to every speaker. This is particularly true for younger speakers who are bilingual or Spanish-dominant. What I have tried to do is create a list of words and phrases which are widely used and useful for everyday life.

While I have included some Mayanized Spanish words (e.g., *laataa, piitoo, talbes*), the percentage of Spanish words represented in the vocabulary is very low compared to that in current usage even by Maya monolinguals. The reason for this is that the Spanish words are the easiest thing in the language to figure out. I have included hybridized expressions that mix Maya words and inflections with Spanish (e.g., *maldisyontik, mu' baler mixba'al, kensa biixi', chinga'an*).

Please note that the latter means 'broken' or 'smashed' and not 'fucked' as one might expect. This usage apparently arose from the Mexican custom of saying *¡Chinga!* 'Fuck!' when something breaks. This usage extends to Maya Spanish where *chingar* can be used in expressions like . . . *y lo chingó* '. . . and he smashed it'. However, many readers with an interest, either positive or negative, in such things will note in perusing the glossary that I have included some sexual and scatalogical vocabulary. There are several reasons for this. First, I consider such terms as part of the basic vocabulary of any language because they do represent a nearly daily, nearly universal part of human existence. The practice of avoiding them in materials dealing with practical language learning is, it seems to me, absurd. Secondly, by addressing the issue directly I hope to satisfy and thereby thwart that immature part of my audience with an abnormal fascination with such terminology. In glossing such terms in English and Spanish, I have given both an ordinary term and an elevated term. This is because the practice of euphemisms, mostly neoclassical, to describe things in a "polite" way does not exist in Maya. Therefore, the Maya word is the equivalent of both. Finally, there is a system of sexual double entendre (*baaxal t'aan*), used primarily by Maya males, which I have not included here (although one example was given in the Travel section above) simply because I don't think that there is too much danger of your being misunderstood. Some discussion of this kind of banter is given in Hanks' *Referential Practice* (p. 120 ff.).

The alphabetical order in the glossary generally follows the usual order of the roman alphabet, but readers should note two ways in which the order differs from the usual practice in English. First, the consonantal digraphs (two letters representing one sound, e.g., *ch* and *ts*) are treated as units, as in Spanish, and not compositionally, as in English. Thus, *ts* is a separate letter that follows *t* instead of being set between *to* and *tu*. The glottalized sounds marked with a glottal stop following the corresponding plain consonant are likewise a distinct letter; thus, *p'* entries follow all *p* entries. With the vowels, all four types (short, long, interglottalized, and postglottalized) of any particular vowel quality (e.g. *o, oo, o'o, o'*) are treated as a unit *o*. Ordering within the unit is the one just given above. Thus, *kooch* 'broad' precedes *koh* 'tooth, beak' instead of following it, as it would in English alphabetization.

A word about verb forms is necessary. I have used the verb stem with the incompletive ending, if any, as the lexical form. Other forms are generally predictable from these. I have also tried to give major anomalous forms (e.g., *suut* and its completive *suunahi*). There are, however, some rather dicey systems of subregularities, i.e., patterns that hold for a relatively small number of verbs (cf. English *sing, ring, swim*, etc.). Refer to the grammatical materials listed in the bibliography for details.

The root forms of the basic inalienably possessed nouns (see Grammar) have been used as the lexical entries. The reader needs to remember that Maya speakers do not use them that way. In mentioning the terms, it is customary to use the form possessed for 'your'; e.g., *ook* 'foot' would be discussed by the Maya as *a wook* 'your foot'. For compounds, however, I have given the possessed form to show the construction (e.g., *u muuk' a wook* 'your thigh', literally 'its strength your foot'.

The observation made in the chapter on pronunciation that there is in Maya a fair amount of variation in pronunciation of some words bears reiterating here. The most difficult area is the length and glottalization of vowels. I have tried to balance my elicitation of pronunciation from the native speakers in the area where I work (eastern Yucatan and central Quintana Roo) with the modern variants given in the Cordemex dictionary. In no case should the representation given here be considered definitive, and you should be prepared to try to sort things out as you hear them used by native speakers.

In cross-checking Maya words from the English-Maya vocabulary, you must remember that the entry may not be under the first word or letter in the expression given. For example, Maya lacks a word with the sense of 'cheap', and the equivalent is therefore the negation of the antonym *ko'oh* 'expensive', i.e, *ma' ko'ohi,* and found under the head entry for *ko'oh* and not under *ma'.* Also, you need always to remember that an initial *w* after *in* and *a* and an initial *y,* especially following a *u,* may need to be ignored to find the entry in the vocabulary; e.g., *in wiits'in* or (*u*) *yiits'in* are found under the letter *i* as *iits'in.*

Some very common grammatical markers such as the pronominal forms and auxiliaries (e.g., *k*), which are covered in the grammar, and some Spanish words (e.g., *restaurante*) used in examples are not included in the vocabularies.

Finally, a word about the English-Maya section of the glossary is necessary. Although I have tried to include most of the English terms from the Maya-English-Spanish section, I have not included the usage examples or the Spanish glosses. When you want to find out how to say something in Maya by looking up the English word, take the Maya equivalents given and look them up in the Maya-English-Spanish section, first for the usage examples and second so that you can check the sense of the Maya word against the Spanish gloss as well.

Maya-English-Spanish Vocabulary

Maya	English	Spanish
A		
abal	(wild) plum	ciruela
aabil	grandchild	nieto
aahal	awaken	despertarse
ahal	awake	despierto
ahlech?	are you awake?	¿estás despierto?
-ak	last	último
anyoak	last year	año pasado
aak	turtle	tortuga
akan	snore	roncar
tun yakan le maako'	the guy's snoring	el hombre está roncando
aktun	cave	cueva
ak'	tongue, vine	lengua, bejuco
aak'	fresh	fresco
aak' bak'	fresh meat	carne fresca
hach aak' le ha'aso'	the bananas are fresh	los plátanos están frescos
aak'ab	night	noche
bin ka aak'abtal	sunset, dusk	anochecer
aal	digit (anatomical)	dedo
u yaal a k'ab	finger	maneto, dedo de la mano
u yaal a wook	toe	dedo del pie

Maya	English	Spanish
aal	heavy	pesado
aalak'	domestic animal, pet	animal doméstico, mascota
a'alik	say (*trans.*)	decirlo
ba'ax ka wa'alik	what do you say? (greeting)	¿qué tal?
aalkab	run	correr
aalkab u man meyah	diligent	diligente
aalkab u meyah	he works quickly	trabaja muy de prisa
kin waalkab	I run	corro
alux	guardian of a milpa	guardián de la milpa
am	spider	araña
amigoo	friend	amigo
aaniis	flavored cane-sugar spirits (commercial)	aguardiente
aantik	help (*trans.*)	ayudarlo
aantah	helper	ayudante
anyo	year	año
arux	guardian of a milpa	guardián de la milpa
asta	until	hasta
asukaar	sugar	azucar

Maya	English	Spanish
atan	wife	esposa
in watan	my wife	mi esposa
awat	cry, yell	gritar, dar gritos
aax	wart	verruga
ayik'al	rich	rico
aayin	crocodile	caimán

B

baab	swim, paddle	nadar, remar
babahki	crowded, well-stocked	atestado, bien surtido
babahki le restaurano'	the restaurant is crowded	hay mucha gente en el restaurante
babahki le tyendao'	the store is well-stocked	está bien surtida la tienda
bach	chachalaca (bird)	chachalaca
baahux	how much (does it cost)?	¿cuánto (cuesta)?
baak	horn, bone	cuerno, hueso
bakal	cob	hueso del maíz, elote
bak'	meat	carne
bak'el yit	ass	nalga
u bak'el wakax	beef	carne de res
ba'al	thing	cosa

Maya	English	Spanish
balam	guardian of the forest	guardián del bosque
baalche'	mead, fermented honey drink (traditional)	
ba'alche'	wild animal	animal silvestre
baler	value	valer
mixtun baler	it's useless, worthless	no vale nada
mu' baler mixba'al	it's useless, worthless	no vale nada
banda	place, area	parte, banda
te'bandao'	in that area	en esa parte
waybandae'	around here, in this area	en esta parte
bat	hail	granizo
baat	axe, hatchet	hacha
batea	washing trough	batea
ba'te'el	fight, problem	pelear, problema
hach yah le ba'te'elo'	it's a difficult problem	el problema es muy duro
tin ba'te'el yetel in sucu'un	I'm fighting with my big brother	estoy peleando con mi hermano mayor
ba'ax	what?	¿qué?
ba'ax k'in	what day?, when?	¿qué día?, ¿cuándo?

Maya	English	Spanish
ba'ax ora	what time? when?	¿qué hora?, ¿cuándo?
ba'axten, ba'en	why?, what for?	¿por qué?
baaxal	play (*intrans.*), joke, amuse	jugar, bromear, divertir
baaxtik	play (*trans.*), use	jugarlo, usarlo
baaxal t'aan	joke, pun	chiste, retuécano
biix ku baaxta'al lelo'	how do you use that?	¿cómo se usa eso?
min kanik baaxtik le aparato'	I don't know how to use the device	no sé usar el aparato
beech'	quail	codorniz
beh	road, trail	camino
sak beho'ob	unpaved roads	caminos blancos
behla'(e')	today, nowadays	hoy
behla'ak	earlier today	hoy anteriormente
bek'ech	slender	delgado
beel	road, matter, affair	camino, asunto
biix a beel(e'ex)	how are you?	¿qué tal?
ts'okol beel	marry, marriage	casarse, casamiento, boda
tun ts'okol in beel	I'm getting married	me voy a casar

Maya	English	Spanish
beora	now	ahora
beorita	right away	ahorita
beoritasa	immediately	en seguida
beetik	do	hacer
he' u beeta'ale'	if possible	si se puede
hu' beeta'ale'	it is possible	es posible
mixtaan u beeta'al	it isn't possible	no es posible
beya'	this way	así
beyo'	that way	así
bey ku beeta'ala'	this is how it's done	así se hace
hach beyo'	perfect!	¡perfecto!
beyts'abile'	maybe, possible	quizás, posible
beyts'abile' kin suut saamal	maybe I'll come back tomorrow	es posible que regrese mañana
bik	be careful	cuida
bik lubkech	watch you don't fall!	¡cuida que no te caigas!
bik'ix	when	cuando
bin	go	ir(se)
binaha'an	he's gone	se fué
bi(n)kahen	I am going to	me voy a
———	———	———
ko'ox (tuun)	let's (go)!	¡vámonos!

Maya	English	Spanish
xi'ik	go (*subj.*)	vaya
bisik	take (*trans.*)	llevarlo
bis a koone	take it to sell!	¡llévelo! a vender!
bise	take it (away)!	¡llévelo!
biix	how?	¿cómo?
biixi'	what?, how's that?	¿cómo?
he biixilie'	as always	como siempre
biyeho	old	viejo
biyehoyn	I am old	soy viejo
hach biyehoych	you're very old	eres muy viejo
booch'	shawl	rebozo
book	smell, odor	olor
ki', uts u book	it smells good	huele bien
tu', k'as u book	it smells bad	huele mal
u'yik book	smell (*trans.*)	sentir (un olor)
bon	dye, paint	tinta, pintura
bona'an	painted	pintado
bona'an le siyao'	the chair is painted	la silla está pintada
bonik	paint (*trans.*)	pintarlo
tin bonik le naho'	I'm painting the house	estoy pintando la casa
bo'otik	pay (for) (*trans.*)	pagarlo
dyos bo'otik	thank you	¡gracias!

Maya	English	Spanish
box	black	negro
box k'ool	black stew	relleno negro
boxha'	coffee	café
bo'ox	buttocks, ass	nalgas
bo'oy	shadow, shade	sombra
buuche	pickled meat dish	salpicón
buka'ah	what size, quantity?	¿de qué tamaño?, ¿cuanto?
buka'ah naachil a kahal	how far is your town?	¿a qué distancia está tu pueblo?
bukintik	put on (clothes) (*trans.*)	vestirse, ponerlo
bu'ul	bean(s)	frijol(es)
k'oobil bu'ul	bean stew	
but'ik	stuff, pack (*trans.*)	llenarlo, embutirlo
yan a but'ik le saako'	you've got to stuff the bag	tienes que llenar el saco
buts'	smoke (*n.*)	humo
buts'ankil	smoke (*intrans.*)	humear
buts'tik	smoke (as to cure) (*trans.*)	ahumarlo
tun buts'ankil le naho'	the house is smoking	la casa está humeando

Maya	English	Spanish
CH		
chab	anteater	oso hormiguero
chaik	permit, allow (*trans.*)	permitirlo, dejarlo
hu' chabale'	it is allowed	se permite
ku chaik in bin	s/he lets me go	me permite ir
mu chabal	one may not	no se permite
chak	red	rojo, colorado
chaak	rain god, rain	dios de la lluvia, lluvia
tun tal chaak	the rain's coming	viene la lluvia
chaakik	parboil (*trans.*)	sancocharlo
chakmool	jaguar	tigre
chakxiich'	blond, fair	güero
chamal	cigarette	cigarro, cigarrillo
chaambeel	slow	despacio, lento
chan	little, small	pequeño, chico
le chan palo'	the little boy	el chico
cha'an	celebration	fiesta
yan cha'an te kaho'	there's a celebration in the town	hay una fiesta en el pueblo
che'	tree, wood, pole, stick	arbol, madera, palo, vara
hump'el che'	a board	una madera
hunkul che'	a tree	un arbol

Maya	English	Spanish
hunts'it che'	a pole	un palo
hunkuch che'	a load of wood	un cargo de leña
cheba	beer	cerveza
che'eh	laugh	reirse
chen	only	solo
chi'	mouth, opening, edge	boca, orilla
chi'bal	bite	morder
tu chi'en le kano'	the snake bit me	me picó la culebra
chich	strong, tough	fuerte, duro
chich iik'	hurricane	huracán
chiich	grandmother	abuela
chichan	little, small	pequeño, chico, poco
chi'ik	coatimundi	pisote, coatí
chi'ikam	jicama	jícama
chika'an	on, running	prendido, encendido
chika'an le aparato'	the device is on	prendido el aparato
chik'in	west	oeste, poniente
chi(l)tal	lie down	acostarse, echarse (en el suelo)
chilahen	I lay down	me acosté

Maya	English	Spanish
china	orange	naranja dulce
china pah	sour orange	naranja agria
u k'aab china	orange juice	jugo de naranja
chinga'an	broken, busted	quebrado
chinga'an in grabadora	my tape recorder's busted	está rota mi grabadora
chi(n)wol	tarantula	tarántula
chooch	intestines	tripas
chokow	warm, hot (not meteorological)	caliente
chokokintik	heat (*trans.*)	calentarlo
chokotal	become hot	calentarse
chokow pol	crazy	loco
chokwil	heat (not meteorological)	calentura
ma' chokwi'	it's not hot	no está caliente
chowak	long	largo
chowakil	length	largura, longitud
chuuh	water gourd	calabaza para llevar agua
chuuk	charcoal	carbón
chukik	catch (*trans.*)	alcanzarlo, pescarlo
chuka'an	complete, finished	completo
chukbesik	complete, finish (*trans.*)	completarlo, terminarlo

Maya	English	Spanish
chukpachtik	pursue, overtake (*trans.*)	alcanzar al que va adelante
ma' chuka'an a p'ismail a konoli'	the amount you're selling isn't all there	no está completa la medida de lo que vendes
chukwa'	chocolate	chocolate
chumuk	half, middle, center	medio, centro
chumuk aak'ab	midnight	media noche
chumuk k'in	noon	medio día
chunchumuk	fifty-fifty	mitad y mitad
tu chumuk le kaho'	in the middle of town	en el centro del pueblo
chun	stem, base, origin, beginning, trunk	raíz, principio, tronco
chunbesik	begin (*trans.*)	empezarlo, comenzarlo
chunpahal	begin (*intrans.*)	empezar, comenzar
u chun pak'	foundation	cimiento
u chun ha'as	banana stalk	tronco del plátano
chuup	full, swollen	lleno, hinchado
chup(s)ik	fill (*trans.*)	llenarlo, henchirlo
chupe(s)	fill it!	¡llénalo!
chuupul	fill (*intrans.*)	henchirse
chuuy	sew	costurar
chuuyche'	vertical stick wall	bajareque

Maya	English	Spanish
CH'		
ch'achaak	rain ceremony	
ch'a'ik	grab, grasp, take, use, bring (*trans.*)	agarrarlo, llevarlo, usarlo traerlo
ch'a'ik iik'	breathe	respirar
ch'a'ik ool	get tired	cansarse
tin ch'a'ik in wiik'	I'm breathing	estoy respirando
tin ch'a'ik in wool	I'm getting tired	me estoy cansando
ch'aakik	cut with a blow (*trans.*)	cortarlo con un golpe
ch'akik che'	clear brush	cortar monte
ch'amak	fox, coyote	zorro, coyote
ch'e'eh	noise, odor	ruido, olor
hach ch'e'eh	it's noisy	hace mucho ruido
hach ch'e'eh u book lelo'	that really stinks	huele muy mal eso
ch'eel	(blue) jay, fair-complexioned	arrendajo, güero
chan ch'eel	blond child	niño güero
hach ch'eel le chan paalo'	the kid is very fair	es güero el niño

Maya	English	Spanish
ch'e'en	well	pozo
ch'iich'	bird	pájaro
ch'iihil	grow	crecer
ch'iiha'an	grown (up)	crecido
ch'iilankabil	relative	pariente
ch'ilib	twig, toothpick	ramita, palillo de dientes
ch'iin	throw	tirar
ch'iinik	throw stones (at) (*trans.*)	tirarlo
tin ch'iinah le pek'o'	I stoned the dog	le tiré una piedra al perro
ch'o'	rat, mouse	rata, ratón
ch'oom	buzzard	zopilote
ch'omak	fox, coyote	zorro, coyote
ch'oop	blind	ciego
ch'ooy	bucket	cubeta, cubo
ch'u	epiphyte	espilladero, epífita
ch'uhuk	sweet, sugar, fruit	dulce, azúcar, fruta
ch'uktik	spy on, waylay (*trans.*)	espiarlo, acecharlo
ch'uul	moist, wet	mojado
ch'uulik	moisten (*trans.*)	mojarlo
ch'uulul	become moist	mojarse
ch'uupal	girl	muchacha

Maya	English	Spanish
ch'uupul xib	gay, queer	maricón
ch'uuyul	hang, be suspended	colgarse, suspenderse
ch'uykintik	hang (*trans.*)	colgarlo, suspenderlo
hun ch'uuy ha'as	a bunch of bananas	un racimo de plátanos

E

Maya	English	Spanish
e'hoch'e'en	dark	oscuro
e'hoch'e'ntal	become dark	oscurecerse
k'as e'hoch'e'en	fairly dark	medio oscuro
tun ye'hoch'e'ntal	it's getting dark	se oscurece
ek'	star	estrella
eek'	dirty	sucio
eek' in nook'	my clothes are dirty	mi ropa está sucia
eek' le lu'umo'	the floor is dirty	el suelo está sucio
elel	burn	quemarse, arderse
eelel in wo'och	my meal is burned	está quemada mi comida
san eelek	it's burned	está quemado

Maya	English	Spanish
eemel	descend	bajarse
eemen	go down!	¡bája!
ensik	lower (*trans.*)	bajarlo
e'esik	show (*trans.*)	mostrarlo
e'eskuba	show (*refl.*)	mostrarse
tak in we'esik tech	I want to show it to you	quiero mostrártelo
et	with, together (*aux.*)	con, juntos
in wet bin el maako'	the guy's going with me	el hombre va conmigo
in wetmaakin	my buddy	mi compañero
in wetxibil	my companion	mi compañero
tin wetel	with me	conmigo
yetel	with	con
eex	pants	pantalón
yeex ko'olel	panties	pantaleta, calzón(es)

H

Maya	English	Spanish
ha'	water, rain, lake	agua, lluvia, laguna
chokow ha'	hot water	agua caliente
siis ha'	cold water	agua fría
tun k'aaxal ha'	it's raining	está lloviendo
ha'ab	year	año

Maya	English	Spanish
hayp'el a ha'abil	how old are you?	¿cuántos años tienes?
hayp'el ha'ab yan tech?	how old are you?	¿cuántos años tienes?
hun(p'el) ha'ab	one year	un año
oxp'el ha'aben	three years old	tiene tres años
u ha'abil	age	edad
hach	very	muy
hach k'as	horrible	horrible, horroroso
hach ya'ab	much, a lot, enough	mucho, bastante
hach'ik	chew (*trans.*)	mascarlo
haah	true	verdadero
haahil	truth	verdad
hahalki	slimy, slippery	liso, resbaloso
hak'oolal	be afraid	espantarse, tener miedo
mu' hak'al a wool	don't get upset	no te espantes
haal	edge, base, side	orilla, raíz
tu haal le beho'	at the edge of the road	a la orilla del camino
haaleb	paca	tepezcuintle
halibe'	that's it, anyhow	ni modos (*sic*), sin embargo
hanal	eat (*intrans.*)	comer
haanal/hanlil	meal	comida

Maya	English	Spanish
hantik	eat (*trans.*)	comerlo
hanil	clear, clean	claro, limpio, despejado
hanil le kaano'	the sky is clear	está despejado el cielo
ha'as	banana	plátano
hunts'it ha'as	one banana	un plátano
hatsik	divide, leave (*trans.*)	dividirlo, partirlo, quitarlo
hatskab k'iin	early, morning	temprano, la mañana
hats'ik	beat, whip, hit, strike (*trans.*)	golpearlo, azotarlo, pegarlo
u hats' chaak	lightning bolt	rayo de cielo
hats'uts	beautiful, nice	hermoso, bonito
hats'utsil	beauty	belleza
hay	thin, flat, level	delgado, llano, plano
hayam	stone slab	laja
hayk'intik	dry in the sun (*trans.*)	secarlo en el sol
hayk'inta'an	dried	seco
hayk'inta'an le iiko'	the peppers are sun-dried	el chile está secado al sol
haytul	how many (people or animals)?	¿cuántos?

Maya	English	Spanish
hayp'el	how many (things)?	¿cuántos?
he'	egg	huevo
ye'el aak/huh	turtle/iguana egg	huevo de tortuga/ iguana
ye'el toon	balls, testicles	cojones, testículos
he'bik	open (*trans.*)	abrirlo
he'ba'an	be open	abierto
he'bel	open (*intrans.*)	abrirse
ku he'bel le iglesiao'	the church opens	se abre la iglesia
tin he'bik le naho'	I'm opening the house	estoy abriendo la casa
hela'an	distinct, different	distinto, diferente
hela'an le xambo'	the shoes are different	los zapatos son diferentes
tu heel lugar	in another place	en otro lugar
tu heel k'iin	so long!	¡hasta luego!, ¡hasta mañana!
u heel	other, different	otro, diferente
he'la'	here it is, here's ————	aquí tienes, aquí está ————
he'le'	indeed, to be sure, yes	sí, claro
he'lel	rest	descansar
he'skuba	rest oneself (*refl.*)	descansarse

Maya	English	Spanish
tin bin in he'simba	I'm going to rest	me voy a descansar
heets'a'an	fixed, firm	firme, asentado, fundado
hmen	shaman, herbalist	curandero, yerbatero
hooch	harvest	cosecha, cosechar
hoochik	harvest (*trans.*)	cosecharlo
yan in hooch	I have to harvest	tengo que cosechar
hoholki	slippery, slimy	resbaloso, liso
hoholki le kayo'	the fish is slimy	está liso el pez
hoholki le lu'umo'	the floor is slippery	está resbaloso el suelo
hook'ol	go/come out, appear	salir, manifestarse
ho'sapunta	pencil sharpener	sacapuntas
ho'sik	bring out, extract (*trans.*)	sacarlo
tin hook'ol Saki'	I'm leaving for Valladolid	salgo para Valladolid
hool	hole, opening, end	hoyo, hueco, cabo
u hool kah	town entrance	entrada del pueblo
u hool nah	house door	entrada o puerta de la casa

Maya	English	Spanish
ho'ol	head, skull	cabeza, calavera
u ho'ol nah	roof	techo
ho'lyak	yesterday	ayer
homa'	large gourd	jícara grande
hop'	begin, start	empezar
hop' u hanal	s/he begins to eat	empieza a comer
hooykep	lazy	flojo
hooykepech	you're lazy	eres flojo
húchi	scram! (to pigs)	¡vete! (a puercos)
huch'	grind	moler, el molido
bin huch' Hwana	Jane went to the mill	Juana fue a moler
huch' k'u'um	grind (lime-soaked) corn	moler nixtamal
huch'bil	ground	molido
huh	iguana, lizard	iguana, lagartijo
-hul	identical (classifier)	idéntico
huum	make noise	hacer ruido
huum chaak	thunder	trueno
hun-	one	un
hach hump'iit	very little, few	muy poco(s)
huhump' iitil	little by little	poco a poco
hump'el	a(n), one (thing)	un(o) (cosa)
hump'iit	a bit, a little	(un) poco, pocos
humpuli	totally, completely	totalmente, completamente

Maya	English	Spanish
hun	single	solito
hunkul	a(n), one (tree)	un(a) (árbol)
hunts'it	a(n), one (long thing)	un(a) (cosa larga)
huntul	a(n), one (person or animal)	un(a) (persona o animal)
ta hun	you're unmarried	eres solito
tin hun	I'm alone/single	estoy solito
hu'un	paper, book, letter	papel, libro, carta
ts'iib hu'un	writing paper	papelería

I

iib	lima bean	frijol lima, ibes
ich	eye, face	ojo, cara
uts tin wich	I like it	me gusta
iicham	husband	marido, esposo
le iichantsilo'	the husband	el esposo
ich(il)	inside, within, in	dentro
ich kol	in the milpa	en la milpa
ich maya	in Maya	en maya
ichil le naho'	inside the house	dentro de la casa
ichil ti' ten	inside me	dentro de mí
ichkiil	bathe	bañarse
tin bin ichkiil	I'm going to take a bath	voy a bañarme

Maya	English	Spanish
iich'ak	fingernail	uña
ik	pepper	chile, ají
tikin ik	dried pepper	chile seco
iknal	presence, "space"	presencia
ta wiknal	near you, in your presence, in your case, at your place	contigo
tin bin iknal Pedro	I'm going to Peter's	me voy a la casa de Pedro
tu yiknal	near him/her/it	con él/ella
iik'	wind, air, spirit	viento, aire, espíritu
chich iik'	storm, hurricane	tormenta, huracán
ilik	see (*trans.*)	verlo
ile	see it!	¡vélo!
ile Pedro	see Pedro!	¡ve a Pedro!
iim	teat, bosom, breast	seno, teta, pecho
chuup u yiim	her teats are full	sus senos están llenos
i'nah	seed	simiente, semilla
iipil	native woman's dress	huipil
is	sweet potato, yam	camote
it	anus, asshole	ano

Maya	English	Spanish
u bak'el it	buttocks, ass	nalga
its	resin, rust	resina o leche de árbol, oxidado
u yits in maskab	my machete is rusty	está oxidado mi machete
yits ya'	chicle	chicle
iits'in	younger sibling	hermano menor

K

ka'	and, when, that (*conj.*)	y, cuando, que
ka'	metate	metate
ka'-	two	dos
ka'pul	two times, twice	dos veces
ka'p'el	two (things)	dos
ka'tul	two (people and animals)	dos
le ka'peeli	both	ambos
kaa'	again (*aux.*)	otra vez, de nuevo
ka'teen	again	otra vez, de nuevo
kab	world	mundo
yok'ol (le) kab(o')	all over the world	sobre el mundo
kaab	bee, honey	abeja, miel de abeja
ka'beh	day after tomorrow	pasado mañana
kaabal	(be)low	(a)bajo

Maya	English	Spanish
tin weemel kaabal	I'm going down lower	voy más abajo
kaachik	break (long things) (*trans.*)	quebrar (cosas largas)
kacha'al/ kacha'an	broken, busted	quebrado
ka'chi	earlier, previously	antiguamente, entonces
kaah	town, place	pueblo, lugar, población
in kaahal	my town	mi pueblo
kahchahen Saki'	I lived in Valladolid	viví en Valladolid
kahtal	ranch	rancho
kahtal	live	vivir
kaahsik	begin (*trans.*)	comenzarlo
tin kaahsik in hanal	I begin to eat	comienzo a comer
tin kaahsik in nahil	I'm starting my house	empiezo mi casa
ka'ka't(e')	a little later, afterward, soon	al rato, un poco despues, más tarde
(mas) ka'ka'te'	(see you) later	hasta luego
kal	neck, throat, voice	cuello, garganta, voz

Maya	English	Spanish
ma' kal in kal	I'm hoarse	estoy ronco
kala'an	drunk, intoxicated	borracho
kalchahi in amigoo	my friend got drunk	mi amigo se emborrachó
kaltal	get drunk, drink	emborracharse
kan	snake	culebra
kan-	four	cuatro
kamp'el	four (things)	cuatro
kantul	four (people and animals)	cuatro
ka'nah	tire	cansarse
hach ka'na'nen	I'm real tired	estoy muy cansado
ka'na'an	tired	cansado
kin ka'nah	I'm tiring	me canso
ka'an	sky, heaven	cielo
ka'anche'	raised-bed garden	tablado de palos
ka'anal	up	arriba
tin na'akal ka'anal	I'm going up above	estoy subiendo (arriba)
kanantik	care for, take care of (trans.)	cuidarlo
dyos ku kanantech	may God protect you	que Dios te cuide
kanantaba	take care! be careful!	¡cúidate!

Maya	English	Spanish
kanik	learn, know (*trans.*)	aprenderlo, saberlo
min kanik ook'ot	I don't know how to dance	no puedo bailar
tin kanik maya	I am learning Maya	estoy aprendiendo el maya
ka'nsik	teach (*trans.*)	enseñarlo
ka'nsah	teacher	maestro
kaape	coffee	café
kaax	chicken	pollo
kaldo kaax	consumé	caldo de pollo
tsahbil kaax	fried chicken	pollo frito
xkaax	hen	gallina
kaaxtik	look for, find (*trans.*)	buscarlo, hallarlo
tin kaaxtah in watan	I found my wife	hallé a mi esposa
tin kaaxtik in watan	I'm looking for my wife	busco a mi esposa
kay	fish	pez, pescado
kechtik	trick, fool (*trans.*)	embaucarlo
keeh	deer	venado
ke'el	cold (meteorological)	hace frío
ke'elen	I'm cold	tengo frío
k'as ke'el	cool	medio frío
keleembal	shoulder	hombro

Maya	English	Spanish
kensa	who knows	¡quién sabe!
kensa biixi'	perhaps	tal vez
kensa maax	I don't know who	no sé quién
ketik	start (a fight) (*trans.*)	empezar (una pelea)
min ketik	I'm not starting it	no lo empiezo
tin ketah	I started it	lo empecé
kex	although	aunque
ki'	nice, convenient	bonito, bueno
ki'	tasty	sabroso
hach ki'	it's good (food), tasty	¡es sabrosísimo!
kib	candle	vela, candela
ki'ichpam	good-looking	hermoso, guapo
kih	sisal hemp, agave	henequén, maguey
kiik	elder sister	hermana mayor
kiimak ool	content, happy	contento, feliz
kiimak in wool	I'm content, happy	estoy contento, feliz
kimil	die	morir
kimen	dead	muerto
kinsik	kill (*trans.*)	matarlo
kinbesik	hurt (*trans.*)	herirlo
kinpahal	hurt oneself	herirse
kinpahen	I'm hurt	estoy herido

Maya	English	Spanish
kirits'	squeak	chirriar
kis	flatulence, fart	pedo
kiskuba	flatulate, fart	echar pedos
kisiin	devil	diablo
kitam	peccary, wild boar	jabalí, puerco del monte
kiwi'	annatto	achiote
kooch	broad	ancho
koh	tooth, beak (of a bird)	diente, pico
koh	puma	puma, jaguar
ko'oh	expensive	caro
ma' ko'ohi'	cheap	barato
kook	deaf	sordo
kol	field, farm	milpa
ich kol	in the field	en la milpa
kolnaal	milpa tiller, farmer	milpero
kolik	clear (forest) (*trans.*)	tumbar (monte)
ku kol k'aaxo'ob	he farms in the forest	hace una milpa en el monte
ko'olel	woman	mujer
koolik	pull (*trans.*)	jalarlo
kolo'ohche'	small vertical sticks (of house wall)	bajareque, palos verticales (de la casa)

Maya	English	Spanish
koom	narrow, short	corto
konik	sell (*trans.*)	venderlo
konol	vendor, salesman	vendedor
xkonol	saleswoman	vendedora
kopik	coil (rope) (*trans.*)	enrollar (soga)
koos	falcon	halcón
ko'oten	come! (*imper.* only)	¡ven!
ko'ox (tun)	let's (go)!	¡vámonos!
ko'one'ex	(*pl.*)	
ko'ox hanal	let's eat	¡vamos a comer!
kuch	burden, load, obligation, fault	carga, cargo, culpa
kuchik	carry (*trans.*)	cargarlo, llevarlo
u kuchil huch'	milling place	lugar de moler, molina
kuuk	elbow	codo
ku'uk	squirrel	ardilla
-kul	tree (classifier)	árbol
kulal	sit	sentar
kula'an	seated	sentado
kulen(e'ex)	be seated!	¡siente(n)se!
ku(l)tal	sit down	sentarse
kuts	oscelated (wild) turkey	pavo del monte
kuxtal	live	vivir

Maya	English	Spanish
kuxa'an	alive, living	vivo, viviente
kuux	what about ——?	¿y ——?
kuux tech	what about you?	¿y tú?
kwatro narises	fer-de-lance	cuatro narices

K'

Maya	English	Spanish
k'ab	hand, arm, branch	mano, brazo, rama
u k'ab che'	tree branch	rama de árbol
k'aab	juice, broth	jugo, zumo, caldo
u k'aab china	orange juice	jugo de naranja
u k'aab kaax	chicken broth	caldo de pollo
k'aaba'	name	nombre
ba'ax/biix a k'aaba'?	what's your name?	¿cómo te llamas?
k'abeet	necessary	necesario
k'abka'	metate and mano	metate y mano
k'aah	bitter	amargo
k'ahol	know someone	conocerlo
a k'ahoten?	do you remember me?	¿me reconoces?
k'ahot(ik)	know, recognize, remember (trans.)	conocerlo, reconocerlo, recordarlo
min k'aholi'	I don't know him/her	no lo conozco
k'aak'	fire	fuego, candela

Maya	English	Spanish
k'a'bil	roasted, grilled	asado
k'a'bil bak'	grilled meat	carne asada
k'a'atik	grill, roast (*trans.*)	asarlo
k'alik	close (*trans.*)	cerrarlo
k'aalal	close (*intrans.*)	cerrarse
k'ala'an	closed	cerrado
k'a'am	strong, harsh	recio, fuerte
hach k'a'am iik'	the wind is strong	el viento es muy recio
k'amas	termite	termita
k'amik	receive, obtain	recibir, obtener
k'an	yellow, ripe	amarillo, maduro
k'an u yich on	the avocados are ripe	los aguacates son maduros
k'aan	hammock	hamaca
k'anche'	stool, chair	banquillo, silla
k'anho'ol	pillow	almohada
k'ana'an	necessary, important	necesario, importante
hach k'ana'an	it's necessary	es necesario
k'as	bad, evil, somewhat	mal, feo, medio
hach k'as u bin	dangerous	peligroso
k'as ke'el	it's cool	hace medio frío
k'at	gnome, forest spirit	enano mitológico
k'aatik	ask for, ask (*trans.*)	pedirlo, preguntarlo

Maya	English	Spanish
a k'aat(e)?	do you want it?	¿lo quieres?
in k'aat(e)	I want it	lo quiero
in k'aatah u chi'	I asked him something	se lo pregunté
k'aat(ik) chi'	ask	preguntar
k'aatik ti'	ask someone (for) (*trans.*)	pedirlo
k'aax	weed, brush, jungle, forest	yerba, monte, bosque
k'aaxil winik	forest dweller	montesino, campesino
k'axab nak'	belt, strap	cinturón, faja
k'aaxal	rain, precipitate	llover, precipitar
k'aax ha' holyak	it rained yesterday	llovió ayer
k'aaxal ha'	rain	llover, lluvia
k'axche'	bullring (home-made)	plaza de toros
k'aaxik	tie up (*trans.*)	amarrarlo
k'aay	sing, song, music	cantar, canción, música
tun k'aay le ch'iich'o'	the bird is singing	está cantando el pájaro
k'eban	sin, wrong	pecado
k'eban ba'ax ka meetik	what you're doing is wrong	es pecado lo que haces

Maya	English	Spanish
k'eek'en	pig, pork	cochino, puerco
hach k'eek'en le maako'	the guy is really crazy, stubborn	el hombre es muy loco, terco
k'ewel	skin, hide, leather	piel, pellejo, cuero
k'ewel xanab	leather shoe	zapato, guarache
k'exik	change (*trans.*)	cambiarlo
k'eexel	change, exchange	cambiar, trocar
tun k'eexel le ka'ano	the sky is changing	está cambiando el tiempo
k'eyem	corn gruel	pozole
k'eeyik	scold, reprimand (*trans.*)	regañarlo, reñirlo, reprenderlo
ma' k'eeyik le paalo'	don't scold the kid	no le regañas al niño
k'i'ik'	blood	sangre
k'iilkab	hot, humid (weather)	hace calor, sudando
k'as k'iilkab	muggy	medio sudando
k'iin	sun, day, time	sol, día, tiempo
k'iinal	hot, become hot	caliente, calentarse
k'iinam	pain	dolor
k'iinam ho'ol pol	headache	dolor de cabeza
k'i'ix	thorn	espina
k'i'xooch	porcupine	puerco espín
k'ooben	kitchen, hearth	cocina, fogón

Maya	English	Spanish
k'oha'an	sick, pregnant (of women)	enfermo, embarazada
k'oha'nil	illness	enfermedad
k'oha'ntal	become ill	enfermarse
k'ool	stew, broth	guiso, caldo
box k'ool	Yucatecan black stew	relleno negro
k'ono'ch	chin	barbilla
k'oop	gully, ravine	barranca
k'osik	cut with scissors (*trans.*)	cortarlo con tijera
tin k'osik le paalo'	I'm giving the kid a haircut	estoy peluqueando al niño
k'o'ox	wild	bravo, cimarrón, salvaje
k'oxol	mosquito	mosquito, mosco
k'u'	nest	nido
k'ubik	deliver (*trans.*)	entregarlo
k'uchul	arrive	llegar
k'uch ximbal	visit	visita
k'uchul te'lo'	arrive there	llegar allá
k'uchul waye'	arrive here	llegar aquí
san k'uchkech	you're here!	¡ya estás llegando! ¡llegaste!
k'uho'ob	twins	gemelos
k'uk'um	feather	pluma

Maya	English	Spanish
k'ulu'	raccoon	mapache
k'uum	squash, pumpkin	calabaza
k'u'um	hominy	nixtamal
k'uruch	cockroach	cucaracha
k'uuts	tobacco, marijuana	tabaco, marijuana

L

la'achik	scrape, scratch (*trans.*)	rascarlo
yan in la'achik in k'ab	I've got to scratch my arm	tengo que rascarme el brazo
lah	all	todo
lah bino'ob tulakal	all have gone	todos se fueron
laak'	other, spouse, relative	otro, esposo, pariente
in laak'	my relative, spouse	pariente, esposo
lak'tsil	family, relative	familia, pariente
tulakal in lak'tsilo'ob	all my relatives	todos mis parientes
u laak' bini	the other guy left	el otro se fue
lak'in	east	este, oriente
laal	nettles	ortiga, chichicaste
laataa	tin can	lata
la'tene	therefore	por eso

Maya	English	Spanish
laylie	the same (thing), always	igual, lo mismo, siempre
laylie kin wenel tardeo'	I always sleep in the afternoon	siempre duermo en la tarde
le'	leaf	hoja
u taan u le'	the bundle of leaves	el haz de hojas
lela'	this (one)	éste, ésta
lelo'	that (one)	ése, ésa
chen lelo'	that's it, nothing else	sólo eso, nada más
lelo' ma' u pahtal kuchik	you can't carry that	eso no lo puedes cargar
le ken . . . -e'	as soon as	cuando
le ken k'uchuk le maake'	as soon as the guy got here	cuando llegue el hombre
liik'il	rise, arise	levantarse
ku li'skuba	he's getting ready	se alista, se prepara
liik'a'an	he's gotten up	se ha levantado
li'saba	get ready!	!alístate!
li'sik	raise, prepare, make ready (*trans.*)	levantarlo, prepararlo, alistarlo
loob	injury, wound, accident, misfortune, untidy	daño, herida, accidente, desgracia, lóbrego
hach loobech tin wich	I hate you	te aborrezco mucho

Maya	English	Spanish
loobil	evil, sin, ruin	maldad, pecado, ruin
lokansbil	boil	hervir
lol	flower, rose	flor, rosa
loxik	punch (*trans.*)	pegarlo con puño cerrado
luub	league	legua
lubul	fall	caerse
luch	tree gourd	jícara, calabaza de árbol
u luch sa'	a gourd of atole	una jícara de atole
lukum	earthworm	lombriz de tierra
luk'ul	leave, escape, flee	quitarse, librarse, huirse
lu'sik	cause to leave (*trans.*)	hacerlo quitar/ir
lu'um	soil, ground, dirt, land	tierra, suelo
hump'el xet' lu'um	a piece of land	pedazo de terreno, lote
luunaa	moon	luna

M

ma'	no, not, without	no, sin
ma' teni'	not me	no soy yo, no fuí yo

Maya	English	Spanish
ma' in wohli'	I don't know	no lo sé
ma'tech	no indeed	no
machik	grab, grasp (*trans.*)	agarrarlo, asirlo
mahan	step-(relation)	prestado
in mahan its'in	my kid step-brother/sister	mi hermanastro/a
in mahan mamah	my step-mother	mi madrastra
mahantik	lend, loan (*trans.*)	prestarlo
mahanten taak'in	lend me some money!	¡présteme dinero!
maak	person	persona, gente
makalmak	which?	¿cuál?
makan	bower, arbor	enramada
mak'antik	make by hand, prepare (*trans.*)	hacerlo a mano, prepararlo
tin mak'antik in wo'och	I'm fixing my meal	estoy haciendo mi comida
maldisyon(ar)tik	curse (*trans.*)	maldecirlo
ma'aloob	o.k., good, well	bien, correcto, adecuado
mamah	mother	mamá
mamich	grandmother	abuela
mansik	pass (*trans.*)	pasarlo
maan	pass by	pasar

Maya	English	Spanish
maan taanil	go ahead	adelantarse, pasarse adelante
mansik aak'ab	spend the night	pasar la noche
tak a maan taanil	you want to go ahead	quieres pasar adelante
manik	buy (*trans.*)	comprarlo
mas	more	más
masewal	Indian, Maya	indígena, mazehual, maya
maskab	machete, iron	machete, hierro
maskabil xamach	iron griddle	comal de hierro
ma'tan	won't	no
ma'tan in beetik	I won't do it	no on hago
maax	who	quien
he' maaxe'	whoever	cualquier persona
maaxi'	who?	¿quien?
mehen	small, little	pequeño, chico
meek'ik	embrace (*trans.*)	abrazarlo
tin meek'ah in suku'un	I gave my brother a hug	abrazé a mi hermano
meerech	lizard (species)	lagartija (una especie)
me(n)tik	make (*trans.*)	hacerlo
me'ex	beard, moustache	barba, bigote
meyah	work	trabajo, trabajar

Maya	English	Spanish
mina'an	there is no(ne)	no hay ningun(a)
na'am	there is no(ne)	no hay ningun(a)
mis	cat	gato
miis	broom	escoba
miistik	sweep, clean (*trans.*)	barrerlo, limpiarlo
mix	not, neither	ni, tampoco
mixba'al	nothing	nada
mixbik'in	never	nunca
mixmaak	no one	nadie
mixtu'ux	nowhere	en ninguna parte
mots	root	raíz
much	toad, frog	sapo, rana
mukik	bury (*trans.*)	enterrarlo, sepultarlo
muuk'	force, forceful	fuerza, fuerte
u muuk' a k'ab	upper arm	brazo
u muuk' a wooc	thigh	muslo
mul	together	juntos
ko'ox mul hook'ol	let's start out together	vamos a salir juntos
muul	hill, pyramid	cerro, pirámide
muxbil	ground (into meal)	molido
mu(n)yal	cloud	nube

Maya	English	Spanish
N		
naach	far, distant	lejos
naach (ti') Saki'	far from Valladolid	lejos de Valladolid
naach ti' waye'	far from here	lejos de aquí
naachil	distance	distancia
nah	house	casa
nahil	home, building	casa, edificio
u nahil koonol ts'aak	pharmacy	farmacia
na'akal	climb, get up in/on	subir
nak'	stomach, belly	barriga, panza
nal	ear of corn	elote
na'am	there is no(ne)	no hay
napulak	right away	en seguida
na'atik	understand (*trans.*)	entenderlo, comprenderlo
min na'atik	I don't get it	no entiendo
naats'	near	cerca
naats' (ti') waye'	near here	cerca de aquí
naats' (ti) Saki'	near Valladolid	cerca de Valladolid
naats'al	approach	acercar
naats'ik	approach (*trans.*)	acercarlo
naats'kuba	approach (*refl.*)	acercarse
naay	dream	soñar
tan a naay	you're dreaming	estas soñando
neh	tail	cola, rabo

Maya	English	Spanish
neek'	seed	pepita, semilla
neen	mirror	espejo
ni'	nose	nariz
xni' pek'	hot sauce (literally, dog's nose)	salsa picante
nikte'	flower	flor
nikte' ha'	waterlily	nenúfar, flor de agua
niix	slope, incline, steep	cuesta, ladera, inclinado
hach niix le muulo'	the pyramid is very steep	está muy inclinada la pirámide
nixik	tilt (*trans.*)	inclinarlo
niixil kab	depth	fondo
u niix le muulo'	the slope of the pyramid	la cuesta de la pirámide
yan a nixik le meesao'	you've got to tilt the table	tienes que inclinar la mesa
no'oh	right	derecha
no'ha'an	to the right	a la derecha
tin no'h k'ab	in my right hand	en la mano derecha
nohoch (pl. nukuch)	big, large	gran, grande(s)
nohchil	boss	jefe
nohoch winik/koolel	old man/woman	viejo/vieja
nohochil	size	tamaño

Maya	English	Spanish
nohol	south	sur
nookoy	cloudy, overcast	nublado
nokoytal	become overcast	nublarse
nook'	clothes, clothing, dress	ropa
nook'ol	worm	gusano
nuuk	big	grande
nuuktak	grown-up, adult	grande, mayor, mayor de edad
nuuktako'ob in paalalo'ob	my kids are grown	mis hijos son grandes
nuukik	answer (*trans.*)	contestarlo, responderlo
nu'kul	tool, utensil, necessity	utensilio, traste, herramiento
nuum	useless, incapacitated	inútil
nuumen	I'm incapacitated	estoy inútil
nuxib	old	viejo, anciano

O

Maya	English	Spanish
ooch	opossum	zorrillo, tlacuache
o'och	meal, dinner	comida
ohel	know (*trans.*)	saberlo, conocerlo
oheltik	find out (*trans.*)	reconocerlo, enterarse de

Maya	English	Spanish
ook	foot, leg	pie, pierna
a wook	your foot, leg	tu pie, pierna
okaank'iin	evening	tarde
okol	enter	entrar
oksik	insert, introduce, put (*trans.*)	hacerlo, entrar, introducirlo, meterlo
ookol	steal	hurtar, robar
ooklik	steal (*trans.*)	hurtarlo, robarlo
ookolbil	stolen	robado, hurtado
yooklah in taak'in	he stole my money	me hurtó mi dinero
okom	post, pillar	poste, pilar, horcón
ook'ol	cry, weep	llorar
ma' a wook'ol	don't cry!	¡no llores!
ook'ot	dance, dancing	bailar, baile
taak a wook'ot tin wetel	do you want to dance with me?	¿quieres bailar conmigo?
ool	mind	mente
kiimak in wool	I'm happy	estoy contento
mu' hak'al a wool	don't get upset	no te asustes
siis in wool	I'm relaxed	estoy fresco
siis ool	cool (weather)	fresco
ola	hello	hola
on	avocado	aguacate

Maya	English	Spanish
oop	soursop	anona
oop'	toasted	tostado
tsahbil oop'	corn chips	tostaditos
ora	hour	hora
otoch	home	casa, patria
otsil	poor	pobre
ox-	three	tres
oxp'el	three (animals)	tres
oxtul	three (inanimates)	tres
oxpul	three times	tres veces
oxbeh	day after the day after tomorrow	día después de pasado mañana
oxo'ontik	shuck (corn) (*trans.*)	desgranarlo

P

Maya	English	Spanish
pa'ik	break (*trans.*)	romperlo, quebrarlo
tin pa'ah hump'el baso	I broke a glass	rompí un vaso
pach	back, behind	espalda, lomo, detras de
tu pach le restauranto'	in back of the restaurant	detrás del restaurante
pah	sour, acidic	agrio, ácido
pahtal	be able to	poder
tan u pahtal	can	se puede
mu' pahtal	cannot	no se puede

Maya	English	Spanish
paak	cut brush, clear	chapear
paktik	look (at) (*trans.*)	mirarlo
pakte	look at it!	¡míralo!
pak'	wall (of masonry)	pared (de mampostería)
pak'il nah	masonry house	casa de mampostería
pak'ach	flatten tortillas	tortear
pak'achtik	flatten, pound (*trans.*)	tortearlo, hacerlo
pak'achtik waah	make tortillas	hacer tortillas
pak'achbil waah	tortillas	tortillas
pak'al	sow, plant	sembrar, planta
pak'ik	sow (*trans.*)	sembrarlo
pak'a'an	sown	sembrado
pak'aal	citrus fruit	cítricos
paak'am	prickly pear cactus	nopal, tuna
paal	boy, child, son	niño, hijo
paalalo'ob	children	niños
pamilya	family, wife	familia, esposa
pan (pam)	bread	pan
paanik	scrape, dig (*trans.*)	escarbarlo, cavarlo
paap	burn, bite, hot, spicy	quemar, picar, picante
paapil	sharpness, bite	picante

Maya	English	Spanish
papa ts'ules	pumpkin-seed sauce dish	papa dzules
papah	father, Pope	papá, el pápa
pa'tal	wait	esperar, aguardar
pa't kin wilik	wait and I'll see	espere que vea
pa'ten waye'	wait here	espera aquí
pa'tik	wait for, expect (*trans.*)	esperarlo
paax	music	música
paax k'ool	Yucatecan music	jarana
maya paax	Mayan music	la música de los mayas
pay	incite, call	incitar, llamar
pay wakax	bullfight	torear, corrida de toros
payk'ab	wave, signal (by hand)	señalar, señal
payooch	skunk	zorrillo
paaytik	pull (*trans.*)	jalarlo
tin paaytik ha' ti' ch'e'en	I'm getting water from the well	estoy jalando agua del pozo
pech	tick (insect)	garrapata
pechech	winch	malacate
peek	move, movement	moverse, movimiento

Maya	English	Spanish
peeksik	move (*trans.*)	moverlo
u peek chaac	thunder	trueno
yan u peek le paalo'	the child's going to move	se va a mover el niño
peka'an	lying on the ground, flat	tirado/hechado en el suelo, llano
pek'	dog	perro
pepem	butterfly	mariposa
peets'	trap, snare	trampa
pets'tik	trap (*trans.*)	cazarlo, cogerlo (con trampa)
piib	cooking pit	barbacoa, horno, pib
piibil kaax	baked chicken	pollo pibil
piibil k'eek'en	roasted pork	cochinita piibil
pichi'	guava	guayaba
pich'	thrush (bird)	tordo (cantor)
pik	bedbug	chinche
piik	native slip, dress	enaguas, falda
piim	thick	grueso, gordo
piimpiim waah	fat tortillas	tortillas gruesas
pitik	disrobe (*trans.*)	desnudarse, quitarse
pit a nok'	take off your clothes!	¡desnúdate!
piitoo	flute, whistle	flauta, pito

Maya	English	Spanish
piitoreal	toucan	tucán
pits'	combed cotton	algodón desmotado
pix	case, cover	vaina, cobertura
u pix maskab	machete sheath	vaina de machete
piix	knee	rodilla
pixan	soul, spirit	alma, espíritu
pokbil	toasted, roasted	tostado, asado
pok chuuk	grilled (meat, etc.)	asado (carne, etc.)
pol	head	cabeza
u pol nah	roof	techo
polok	fat, thick	gordo, grueso
polkil	thickness	gordura
poos	faded, pale	descolorido, palido, desteñido
hach poos a kamisa	your shirt is faded	tu camisa está desteñida
pot	penetrate, pass through (*trans.*)	penetrarlo, traspasarlo
tin potholtal	I'm getting through the hole	estoy pasando por el hueco
pootoos	photographs	fotos
puch'ik	crush, break, grind	despachurrar, quebrar, moler
puh	pus	pus, materia de llaga
puksik'al	heart	corazón

Maya	English	Spanish
puuk'	cloudy (liquid), muddy	turbio
hach puuk' le ha'o'	the water's cloudy	está turbia el agua
put	papaya	papaya
puuts'	needle	aguja
puuts'ul	escape, get away	escaparse
puuts'i le wakxo'	the cows got away	se escapó el ganado

P'

p'aak	tomato	jitomate
p'atal	remain	quedar
p'aten waye'	stay here	quédate aquí
p'atik	leave (*trans.*)	dejarlo
tin p'atah in sabukan	I left my bag	dejé mi bolsa
p'ektik	hate (*trans.*)	odiarlo
kin p'ektik miso'ob	I hate cats	odio los gatos
p'eka'an	hateful	aborrecido, abominado
-p'el	(inanimate classifier)	
p'isik	measure, weigh (*trans.*)	medirlo, pesarlo

Maya	English	Spanish
p'isik'aan	land unit 20×20 m.	mecate
yan a p'isik le xi'imo'	you've got to weigh the corn	tienes que pesar el maíz
p'o'ik	wash (*trans.*)	lavarlo
p'o'a'al	washed	lavado
p'o'ik k'ab	wash one's hands	lavarse las manos
p'o'ik nu'kul	wash one's equipment	lavar los trastes
p'o'ik nok'	wash clothes	lavar la ropa
p'ook	hat	sombrero
p'uchik	beat, strike (*trans.*)	golpearlo (con palo)
p'uch	bat (*intrans.*)	batear
p'uhul	become angry, get mad	enojarse
ma' a p'uhul	don't get mad	no te enojes, no te molestes
p'uhsik	disturb, bother (*trans.*)	alborotarlo, molestarlo
tun p'uhskech?	does it bother you?	¿te está molestando?
tun p'uhsken	it bothers me	me está molestando

S

sa'	cornmeal beverage	atole
sabak	soot	tizne
saabin	weasel, ferret	comadreja

Maya	English	Spanish
sabukan	sack, bag	bolsa, morral
sahak	be afraid	tener miedo
hach sahken	I'm really scared	tengo much miedo
ma' ch'a'ik sahkil	don't be afraid	no tengas miedo

sahbesik	frighten, scare
	  (*trans.*)
		asustarlo,
		  espantarlo

sahkil	fear	miedo, temor

tan a sahbesik le
    wakxo'obo'
	you're scaring the
	  cattle
		estás espantando el
		  ganado

sahkab, saskab	crushed limestone	roca calcárea de- leznable, sascab
sak	white, clean	blanco, limpio
sak ha'	pure water	agua limpia
saka'	cornmeal beverage	atole con cáscara
sakan	cornmeal, corn flour	masa de maíz
Saki'	Valladolid	Valladolid
Saki'il	from Valladolid	vallisolitano
sak'	itch, itching	comezón
sak' in paach	my back itches	tengo comezón en la espalda
sak'en	I itch	tengo comezón
saak'	locust	langosta de tierra
saal	light (weight)	ligero, no pesado
sam	just	al cabo de un rato

Maya	English	Spanish
san k'uchken	I've arrived, I'm here!	¡ya llegué!
saame	ready!	¡ya! ¡listo!
saamal	tomorrow	mañana
asta saamal	see you tomorrow!	¡hasta mañana!
saamal okaank'iine	tomorrow evening	mañana por la tarde
sansamal	daily, constantly	diario, cada día
saampol, saamho'ol	tayra	oso colmenero
saas	clear	claro
saasil	light (*n.*)	luz
saastal	become light, dawn	amanecer
u saas hmen	divining crystal	cristal del curandero
saatal	get lost, disappear	desaparecerse
saat in reloh	my watch is lost	se me perdió el reloj
saata'an	lost	perdido
saaten tin beh	I lost my way	perdí el camino
saatik	lose (*trans.*)	perderlo
tan a saatal	are you lost?	¿estás perdido?
tin saatah in reloh	I lost my watch	perdí mi reloj
sats'ik	stretch, extend (*trans.*)	estirarlo
sayab	spring, fountain	ojo de agua, fuente

Maya	English	Spanish
sayap ha'	spring, well	ojo de agua, pozo
seeb	quick	rápido
ka seebak a suut waye'	you should hurry back	debes de regresar rápido
seeb in hook'ol	I'm leaving in a hurry	salgo de prisa
seeb u meyah	diligent	diligente
seebak	quick	rápido
seeba'an	quickly	presto
segirtik	continue (trans.)	seguirlo
ko'ox segirtik saamal	let's continue it tomorrow	vamos a seguirlo mañana
sen	extremely (evaluates quantity)	-ísimo
sen uts, sen ma'aloob	super	buenísimo
se'en	cough, cold	toser, catarro
yan tech se'en	have you got a cold?	¿tienes catarro?
seerbeesa	beer	cerveza
si'	firewood	leña
sihil	be born, birth	nacer, nacimiento
sihen waye'	I was born here	nací aquí
siik	give (as a gift) (trans.)	regalarlo
siibil	gift, present	regalo

Maya	English	Spanish
sikil	pumpkin seed, squash seed	pepita de calabaza
siim	snot, mucus	moco
sina'an	scorpion	alacrán
sinik	hang (up) (*trans.*)	guindarlo, colgarlo
tak a sinik a k'aan waye'?	do you want to hang your hammock here?	¿quieres guindar tu hamaca aquí?
sinik	ant	hormiga
si'pil	sin, error, fault	pecado, yerro, culpa
siis	cool, cold (of things)	frío
siis lu'um	fertile soil	tierra fértil
siis in wool	I'm relaxed	estoy fresco
siis ool	pleasant (weather)	fresco
siskuntik	cool (*trans.*)	enfriarlo
siit	straw, reed	popote
siit'	jump, hop	brincar, saltar
san siit'naken	I already jumped	ya brinqué
sohol	plant debris, trash	basura, basura de hojas secas
so'sook'	tangled	enredado
hach so'sook' in ho'ol	my hair is really tangled	está muy enredado mi pelo
sool	shell, husk, bark	cáscara, carapacho, corteza

Maya	English	Spanish
solaar	family land	solar
soots'	bat	murciélago
suhuy	virgin	virgen
suhuy k'aax	virgin forest	monte virgen (nunca labrada)
suhuy paal	maiden	muchacha
suk	tame	manso
hach suk le pek'o'	the dog is quite tame	es muy manso el perro
suuk	custom	costumbre
suuk ten	I'm used to it	estoy acostumbrado
su'uk	grass, hay, weed	zacate
suku'un	big brother	hermano mayor
suum	rope, lasso	soga, lazo
sup'ik	close, block (a road) (*trans.*)	cerarlo, tapar (un camino)
sup'a'an	blocked (with poles)	cerrado (con palos)
suut	return	regresar
san suunaken	I'm already back	ya volví
suunahi	he came back	regresó
sutik	return (*trans.*)	devolverlo
tin sutik a nu'kul	I'm returning your tool	te devuelvo tu herramienta
su'tal	shame, embarrassment	vergüenza

Maya	English	Spanish
su'laki	s/he's ashamed	se avergüenza, tiene vergüenza
xma' su'tal	shameless	sin vergüenza

T

Maya	English	Spanish
ta'	shit, excrement, dung	mierda, excremento, estiércol
a ta'kaba	you defecated	te defecaste
ta' kaax	chicken shit	mierda de pollo
ta'kuba	shit, defecate (*refl.*)	defecarse
u ta' mis	cat shit	mierda de gato
u ta' miis	sweepings	basura barrida
ta'ab	salt	sal
ta'abil bak'	salted meat	carne salada
ta'bsik	salt (meat or fish) (*trans.*)	salar (carne o pescado)
tahal	cook, boil, bake	cocer
tun tahal le piibo'	the pit is cooking	está cociendo en la barbacoa
tak	until, toward	hasta, hacia
tak domingo	until Sunday	hasta el domingo
tak Saki'	toward Valladolid	hacia Valladolid
taak	want	querer, tener ganas
taak in kanik le mayao'	I want to learn Maya	quiero aprender el maya
ta'akik	care for (*trans.*)	guardarlo, cuidarlo

Maya	English	Spanish
taak'al	stick	pegarse
taak'ik	glue, stick (*trans.*)	pegarlo con pegamento
tak'aan	ripe, cooked	maduro, cocido
taak'in	gold, money	oro, dinero
taak'inal	rich	rico
tal	come	venir
tak	let it come	déjalo venir
tal ich k'aak'	from in the fire	viene del fuego
talbes	perhaps	tal vez
taam	deep, low	profundo, hondo
tamali'	tamale	tamal
taman	sheep, goat	borrego, chivo
taaman	liver	hígado
tamax chi'	omen, prognostication	agüero
taan	before, in front of	delante, enfrente
taanil	front part	parte delantera
u taan a k'ab	the palm of your hand	la palma de la mano
ta'an	lime (calcium carbonate)	cal
tanilí	already	ya
taasik	bring (*trans.*)	traerlo
taas ten	bring it to me	tráemelo
tat(a)	father, grandfather	padre, abuelo

Maya	English	Spanish
nohoch tata	sir, grandfather!	¡señor!, ¡abuelo!
tatich	grandfather	abuelo
taax	flat, level	llano
taaytak	be about to	ya mero, inminente
taaytak k bin	we're about to go	ya mero nos vamos
taaytak u lubul	it's about to fall	ya mero que se cae
te'	here, there	allí
te'la'	here	allá
te'lo'	there	allí
tech	you, to you	tú, a ti
ten	I, to me	yo, a mí
te'ex	to you (all)	a ustedes
ti'	at, to, in, on, with	en, a, con
ti'al	for, belonging to	para, suyo
tihil	dry	secarse
tihsik	dry (*trans.*)	secarlo
tun tihil le iko'obo'	the peppers are drying	se secan los chiles
tun tihsa'al le iko'obo' men in watano'	the peppers are being dried by my wife	mi esposa está secando los chiles
Tiho', Ho'	Merida	Mérida
Ho'il	from Merida	meridano
tikin	dried	seco
tikin xiik'	Yucatecan baked fish	pescado a la moda de Yucatán

Maya	English	Spanish
tiraule	slingshot	resolera, honda
tiital	shake	sacudirse
tiitik	shake (*trans.*)	sacudirlo
tun tiital le meesao'	the table is shaking	se sacude la mesa
tun tiitik le meesao' le pek'o'	the dog is shaking the table	el perro está sacudiendo la mesa
toh	straight, direct	derecho, recto, directo
toh in wool	I'm in good shape	estoy sano y salvo
toh le beho'	the road is straight	el camino es recto
tohol	price	precio
baahux u tohol	how much does it cost?	¿cuál es su precio? ¿cuánto cuesta?
to'ik	wrap, cover, coil, roll up (*trans.*)	envolverlo, cubrirlo, rollarlo
tin to'ik le suumo'	I'm coiling the rope	estoy rollando la soga
to'a'an	wrapped, covered, coiled	envuelto, cubierto, rollado
tokik	take off (*trans.*)	quitarlo
ku tokik in nook'	I take off my clothes	me quito la ropa
took	burn	quemar

Maya	English	Spanish
ba'ax k'in a took	when do you burn your milpa?	¿qué dia quemas tu milpa?
tookik	burn (*trans.*)	quemarlo
tun tookik in nook'	my clothes are on fire	se me está quemando la ropa
tok'tunich	flint	pedernal
toolok	lizard (species)	lagartijo (una especie)
toon	penis, dick	pene, picha
to'on	we, to us	nosotros
topik	fuck (*trans.*)	chingarlo
toot	mute	mudo
tootkook	deaf-mute	sordomudo
tootech wa?	has the cat got your tongue?	¿eres mudo?
tu'ub	forget	olvidar
ma' tu'ubi'	don't forget!	¡no te olvidas!
ma' tuubsik	don't forget it!	¡no lo vayas a olvidar!
tin tu'ubsah in sabukan	I forgot my bag	se me olvidó la bolsa
tu'ub ten	I forgot	se me olvidó
tu'ubsik	forget (*trans.*)	olvidarlo
tu'ubul	forget	olvidarse
tuucha	monkey	mono, chango

Maya	English	Spanish
tuklik	think (*trans.*)	pensarlo
tin tuklik mu'	I don't think it can	estoy pensando que
beeta'al	be done	no va a poder
saamali'	tomorrow	hacerlo mañana
tuukul	think	pensar
tuukul	sad, pensive	triste, pensativo
tulakal	all	todo(s)
tulakal le maako'obo'	all the people	toda las personas
tumben	new	nuevo
a tumben restaurante'ex	your new restaurant	su nuevo restaurante
tumben nok'	new clothes	ropa nueva
u tumben abil	his new grandchild	su nuevo nieto
tumen	because, by	porque, por
tuun	then	entonces
tuunich	rock, stone	piedra
oxp'el tuunich	kitchen fire	fogón, fuego de la cocina
tunkuruchu	owl	buho, tecolote
tuunkuy	heel	tacón, talón
tuunkuy a wooc	the heel of your foot	el talón del pie
tunk'ul	drum	tambor
tuupik	extinguish, put out (*trans.*)	apagarlo, matarlo

Maya	English	Spanish
tuup le k'aak'o'	the fire's gone out	se apagó el fuego
tuupe luuso'	turn off the light!	¡apága la luz!
tuupul	go out	apagarse
turix	dragonfly	cabillito, libélula
tuus	lie, false(hood), make-believe	mentir, mentira
	deceive	fingir, engañar
chen t'aan tuus ba'ax ka wa'alik	what you're saying is a lie	lo que dices es una mentira
tun tuuskech le maako'	the guy's lying to you	te está mintiendo el hombre
tuusik	lie to someone	mentirle a uno
xen a tuuse le paalo'	go lie to the kid	anda a mentir al niño
tusbel	errand	encargo
tusbeltik	order (*trans.*)	mandarlo, ordenarlo
tu'ux	where?	¿dónde?, ¿a dónde?, ¿de dónde?
tu'ux ku yuchul	where does it take place?	¿dónde se realiza?
tu'ux uchi	where did it happen?	¿dónde pasó?

Maya	English	Spanish
tuuxtik	send (*trans.*)	enviarlo
tyempo	time	tiempo

T'

t'aabik	light, ignite (*trans.*)	encenderlo, incendiarlo
t'abe le luuso'	turn on the light!	¡enciende la luz!
yan a t'aabik le k'aak'o'	you've got to light the fire	tienes que encender el fuego
t'aaham	callous, corn	callo
t'aan	language, saying, say	idioma, plática, hablar
ba'ax a t'aan waye'	what are you up to?	¿qué haces por aquí?
kin t'aanik le k'ak'as iik'o'	I call the evil spirits	llamo a los espíritus malos
t'aan iik'	call the spirit	llamar al espíritu
t'aanik	speak (*trans.*)	hablarlo, llamarlo
uts tu t'aan	he likes it	le gusta
t'eel	rooster, cock's comb	gallo, cresta de ave
t'iinil	stiff, tense	tieso, tenso
t'ookik	cut, gather, uproot (*trans.*)	cortarlo, bajarlo, arrancarlo
t'o'ol a pach	spine	espinazo

Maya	English	Spanish
t'oon (a wook)	calf (of your leg)	pantorrilla (de la pierna)
t'ooxik	share, divide up (*trans.*)	repartirlo, distribuirlo
tin t'ooxik le seerbeesao'	I am dividing up the beer	estoy repartiendo la cerveza
t'ubik	sink, submerge (*trans.*)	hundirlo, sumirlo
ma' a t'ubkaba ich ha'	don't go underwater	no te sumejas en el agua
t'uba'an	sunken	hundido, sumido
t'u'ul	rabbit	conejo
t'uup	smallest part, youngest brother	el menor, hermano menor
t'uupil yaal a k'ab	your little finger	el meñique
u t'uupil in wiits'in	my youngest brother	mi hermano menor
t'uut'	parrot	loro, perico

TS

tsab	rattle of a snake	cascabel de víbora
tsab kan	rattlesnake, Pleiades	serpiente de cascabel, Pléyades
tsahik	fry (*trans.*)	freirlo
tsahbil	fried	frito

Maya	English	Spanish
tsahbil kaax	fried chicken	pollo frito
tsaats	(animal) fat	unto, lo gordo de la carne
tsaypachtik	follow (*trans.*)	seguirlo
yan a tsaypachtik	you've got to follow it	tienes que seguirlo
tseel	side	lado
tu tseel le k'ino'	in the afternoon	en la tarde
tu tseel le muulo'	beside the pyramid	al lado de la pirámide
tselik	remove (*trans.*)	quitarlo
tselik k'i'ix	remove thorns	quitar espinas
tseentik	feed (*trans.*)	darle la comida
yan u tseentik ya'abkach winik don Lor	Don Lorenzo's going to feed a lot of people	don Lorenzo va a dar de comer a mucha gente
tsikbal	chat	platicar
tsikbatik	show, tell (*trans.*)	mostrarlo, platicarlo
tsikbatik uchben ba'alo'ob	tell stories	contar cuentos o cosas antiguas
yohel u tsikbate uchben ba'alo'ob le nohoch maako'	the old guy can tell stories	el viejo sabe cuentos

Maya	English	Spanish
tsiimin	horse	caballo
tso'	tom turkey	macho de pavo
tsool	put in order (*trans.*)	ordenarlo
tsoolik	explain (*trans.*)	explicarlo, ordenarlo
tsool ten biix ku meeta'al	tell me how to do it	explícame cómo se hace
tso'ts	hair	pelo
u tso'tse a ho'ol	hair	cabello
tsuub	agouti	agutí

TS'

ts'aak	medicine	medicina
ts'aak se'en	cold medicine	medicina para catarro
ts'aakik	heal (*trans.*)	curarlo
ts'ats'aak	doctor, physician	doctor, médico
ts'ats'	water hole	aguada, laguneta
ts'a'ay	fang	colmillo
ts'iib	write, writing	escribir, escritura
tin ts'iitik in k'aba beya'	I write my name like this	así se escribe mi nombre
ts'iiboltik	imagine (*trans.*)	imaginarlo
ts'ii(b)tik	write (*trans.*)	escribirlo
tun ts'iiboltik waba'ax	he's imagining something	está imaginando algo

Maya	English	Spanish
ts'ik	give, put (*trans.*)	darlo, ponerlo
ts'a ten	give me———!	¡déme———!, ¡pónme———!
ts'aab	it was given, put	fué dado, puesto
ts'iik	left	izquierdo
ts'iika'an	to the left	a la izquierda
ts'iik(a'an) k'ab	left hand	mano izquierda
ts'ikik	shave (*trans.*)	afeitarlo
ts'ika'an	shaven	afeitado
ts'iis	fuck, copulate	chingar, copular
ts'ook	done, ready, end	hecho, listo, fin
chen ts'ookok	when it's done, then	cuando termina, después, entonces
tun ts'okol in beel	I'm getting married	me estoy casando
ts'ok in hanal	I already ate	ya comí
ts'ooken	I am done, ready	estoy terminando, listo
ts'okol beel	get married, marriage, wedding	casarse, casamiento, boda
ts'oksik	finish (*trans.*)	terminarlo
ts'o'om	brains	sesos
ts'oon	gun, firearm, hunt	escopeta, arma de fuego, cazar

Maya	English	Spanish
tin bin ts'oon	I'm going hunting	voy a cazar
ts'oonik	shoot (*trans.*)	dispararlo, tirarlo
ts'oonol, ts'oonero	hunter	cazador
ts'onot	sinkhole	cenote
ts'oy	scar	cicatriz
ts'oya'an	skinny	flaco
ts'ul	foreigner, stranger, white man	extranjero, ladino
yohel maya le ts'ulo'	the white guy knows Maya	el blanco sabe maya
ts'unu'un	hummingbird	colibrí
ts'u'uts'	suck, smoke, kiss	chupar, fumar, besar
ma' ts'u'uts'	no smoking	no fume
ts'u'uts'ik	suck, smoke, kiss (*trans.*)	chuparlo, fumarlo, besarlo
ts'u'uy	tough, leathery	coriáceo, duro
hach ts'u'uy u pol Hwan	John is really dumb	Juan es muy tonto

U

uuchben	old, ancient	antiguo
le uuchben maako'obo'	the ancient Maya	los antigüos

Maya	English	Spanish
uuchilak	previously	anteriormente
uuchul	happen	pasar, suceder
uuchak	may it be so!	¡ojalá!
uuchak in suut tu laak' anyo	I hope to come back next year	ojalá que regrese el próximo año
uukum	dove	paloma
uk'	louse	piojo
uk'ah	thirsty	sed
uk'ahen	I'm thirsty	tengo sed
uk'ul	drink, have breakfast	beber, tomar, desayunar
uk'ik	drink (trans.)	tomarlo, beberlo
uulum	turkey	pavo
urich	(land) snail	caracol (de tierra)
us	gnat	zancudito, jején
uustik	blow (trans.)	soplarlo
p'urustik	inflate (trans.)	inflarlo
uts	good, well	bueno
uts tin wich	I like it	me gusta
utskintik	clean, repair, improve (trans.)	limpiarlo, repararlo, mejorarlo
u'yik/u'bah	hear, feel, smell, listen, perceive (trans.)	oirlo, sentirlo, olerlo, escucharlo, percibirlo
kin wu'yik	I hear it	lo oigo

Maya	English	Spanish
tu yu'bah	he heard it	lo oí
u'ye	listen!	¡oye!

W

Maya	English	Spanish
wa	if, either, or (*interrogative*)	si, o, ¿por ventura?
wa ba'ax	something	algo
wa maax	someone	alguien
wa tu'ux	somewhere	algún lugar
wach	soldier, Mexican	soldado, mexicano
wach'ik	untie (*trans.*)	desatarlo, soltarlo
waah	bread, tortilla	pan, tortilla
ch'uhuk waah	sweet roll	pan dulce
pak'achbil waah	tortilla	tortilla
tsahbil waah	corn chips	tostaditos
wakax	cow, bull, cattle, ox	vaca, toro, ganado, buey
wak'	weave	tejer
tin wak' k'aan	I'm weaving a hammock	estoy tejiendo una hamaca
waak'al	explode, burst	reventar
waak' le boladorao	the rocket exploded	se explotó el cohete
waak'ik	set off (explosive)	prender fuego a (explosivo)

Maya	English	Spanish
yan in waak'ik le boladorao	I'm going to set off the rocket	voy a reventar la voladora
wal(e')	perhaps, maybe	tal vez, puede ser, quizá
tun wenel wale'	I guess he's sleeping	quizá esté durmiendo
wa'tal	stand up, stop	poner de pie, parar
ma' a wa'tal	don't stand there, go on!	¡no te páres!
wa'bal	stopped, on foot, not moving	parado, de pie, inmóvil
wa'akuba	stand (*refl.*)	pararse
wa'lahen waye'	I stood here	paré aquí
wa'alen	stop!	¡alto! ¡párate!
wats'ik	bend (ears of corn) (*trans.*)	doblar (el maíz)
wats'a'an	bent ears	las cañas dobladas
wawa	bus	autobus
waay	wizard	brujo
u meyah xwaay	witchcraft	brujería
xwaay	witch	bruja
wayak'	dream	soñar, sueño
tin k'as wayak'	I'm having a nightmare	tengo una pesadilla
tun wayak' leeti'	he's dreaming	está soñando

Maya	English	Spanish
waye'	here	aquí
wayile'	local, native	de aquí
wayileche'	you're from here	eres de aquí
xwaye'	just (about) here	aquí
wech	armadillo	armadillo
weekik	spill (*trans.*)	derramarlo
weeka'an	spilled	derramado
weekik ha'	spill liquid	derramar líquido
wenel	sleep	dormir
wi'ih	hungry	hambre
ts'oken wi'htal	I'm hungry	tengo hambre
wi'hen	I'm hungry	tengo hambre
winik	person, man	persona, hombre
winklil	body	cuerpo
wiix	urine, urinate, piss	orín, orinar
woolis	round	redondo
wool a k'ab	fist	puño
wuuts'ik	fold, bend (*trans.*)	doblarlo, plegarlo

X

xaache'	comb	peine
kin xaachetik in pol sansamal	I comb my hair every day	me peino el pelo diariamente
xaachetik	comb, brush (one's hair) (*trans.*)	peinarse (el pelo)

Maya	English	Spanish
xak	small basket	canasta pequeña
xa'ak'tik	mix (*trans.*)	mezclarlo, revolverlo
xamach	griddle for tortillas	comal
xaman	north	norte
tun tal xaman ka'an	it's going to get cold	viene el frío del norte
xaman ka'an	north wind	cierzo, viento del norte
xan	also	también
bey xan tech	you too	igualmente
mix xan ten	me neither	ni yo tampoco
ten xan	me too	yo también
xa'an	thatch palm	guano, palmo
xa'nil nah	thatched house	casa de paja
xa'nil p'ook	straw hat	sombrero de paja
xanab	shoe, sandal, footwear	zapato, guarache
xambo'ob	shoes	zapatos
xaanal	be late	tardarse
tak a xaantal waye'	do you want to stick around here?	¿quieres tardarte aquí?
xaanlahen in bin	I was late in going	me tardé en ir
xaantal	stick around	tardarse
xch'uup	woman	mujer
xeh	vomit	vómito, vomitar

Maya	English	Spanish
xet'	bit, piece, portion	pedazo
u xet' waah	a piece of bread	un pedazo de pan
xib	male, man	varón, macho
xibil tso'ts	man's hairstyle	pelo de macho
xi'paal	boy, youth	muchacho, joven
xi'ik	go (*subj.*)	vaya
xen	go!	¡vaya!
xen te'lo'	beat it, scram!	¡váyate!
xi'ik ———	let ———, have ———)	déjalo ———
xi'ik tech utsil	take care, good luck!	que te vaya bien, ¡buena suerte!
xi'ik u bise le chuuko'	have him bring the charcoal	déjalo que traiga el carbón
xiikik	break (*trans.*)	reventarlo
yan in xiikik le baso'	I'm going to break the glass	voy a romper el vaso
xikin	ear	oreja
u xikin k'aak'	spark	chispa
xiik'	wing, armpit	ala, sobaco
yanal xiik'	armpit	sobaco
xi'im	corn	maíz
ximbal	go, walk	andar, caminar
ximbatik	visit (*trans.*)	visitarlo
xiw	(medicinal) herb	hierba (medicinal)
xloob	brush hook	coa

Maya	English	Spanish
xma'	without, lacking	sin, faltando
xma' nook'	naked	desnudo
xnuk	old woman	vieja
xnuk ek'	morning star, Venus	estrella de la mañana, Venus
xook	read, count	leer, contar
xookik	read, count (*trans.*)	leerlo, contarlo
xoolte'	walking stick	bastón
xotik	cut (off) (*trans.*)	cortarlo
xotik si'	cut firewood	cortar leña
xtaabay	ghost, demon	duende, demonio maligno
xtaats'	machete	machete
xu'uk'	landmark	mojón
xul	end	fin, cabo
xul a wool	you wear yourself out	te agotas
xuul	planting stick	sembrador
xunaan	female foreigner, white woman	extranjera, mujer blanca
xun	dear (what husband calls his wife)	cariño
xuupul	consumed, used up	gastarse
tun xuupul	it's being used	se está gastando
xuupi	used up, all gone	se gastó
xux	wasp	avispa

Maya	English	Spanish
xuux	large basket (for gathering corn)	canasta grande
xuxub	whistle	chiflar

Y

Maya	English	Spanish
ya'	sapodilla	zapote
ya'ab	a lot, much	mucho
hach ya'ab	enough	bastante
ma' ya'abi'	not much, little	no mucho, poco
ya'abkach, ya'abo'ob	many	muchos
yah	difficult, hard	difícil, duro
yah kuxlik	it's a hard life	es dura la vida
yah	pain, hurt	dolor, doler
hach yah in nak'	I've got a stomachache	me duele la barriga
yah tu yool	sad, blue	triste
yakuntik	love (*trans.*)	amarlo
cu yakuntik u yatan le maako'	the guy loves his wife	el hombre ama a su esposa
yan	there is, there are	hay
ka yanak	let there be ———	que haya ———
ka yanak a woheltik	I want you to know that ———	quiero que sepas que ———

Maya	English	Spanish
tiyanenKoba'e'	I am there in Cobá	estoy allí en Cobá
yan in ———	I have to ———	tengo que ———, hay que ———
yan in grabadora	I've got my tape recorder	tengo mi grabadora
yan in hok'ol	I've got to leave	tengo que salir
yan in suku'un	I've got a big brother	tengo un hermano mayor
yan ten	I have	tengo
yan ten grabadora	I've got a tape recorder	tengo una grabadora
yanen	I am (located)	estoy
yaanal	below, beneath	abajo, debajo
yaax	before, earlier	antes
yaaxil	first	primero
yaaxil in ximbatik	my first visit	mi primera visita
ya'ax	blue, green	azul, verde
ya'axche'	ceiba tree	ceiba
yeeb	mist	neblina
tun yeeb ha'	it's misting	está neblando el agua
yeh	blade, sharp, pointed	filo, punto, afilado
u yeh kuchiyo	knife blade	filo de cuchillo
yan u yeh	it's sharp	está afilado

Maya	English	Spanish
ye'el aak	turtle egg	huevo de tortuga
ye'el huh	iguana egg	huevo de iguana
ye'el toon	balls, testicles	cojones, testículos
yetel	with, and	con, y
tin wetel	with me	conmigo
yich	fruit	fruta
u yich ha'as	banana fruit	fruto del platano
yich che'	fruit	fruta
yi'h	ripe (for picking)	sazonado
yi'htal	ripen	sazonar
yok'ol	above	encima
yo'om	pregnant	embarazada
yo'om-chaha'an	pregnant	embarazada
yo'om-chaha'an le koolelo'	the lady's pregnant	la mujer está embarazada
yoon	foam	espuma
yuuk	small deer (species)	venado pequeño
yuultik	rub, polish (*trans.*)	frotarlo, bruñirlo
yuum	lord, gentleman	señor
yuumil	owner	dueño
yunchaako'ob	rain spirits	
yuntsil	lord, forest spirit	dueño del monte

English-Maya Vocabulary

English	Maya
A	
able	
be able to	pahtal
about	
be about to	taaytak
above	yok'ol
accident	loob
acidic	pah
afraid	hak'oolal, sahak
afterward	ka'ka't(e')
again	kaa', ka'teen
age	ha'abil
agouti	tsub
air	iik'
alive	kuxa'an
all	lah, tulakal
all gone	xuupi
allow	chaik
it is allowed	hu' chabale'
already	tanilí
also	xan
although	kex
always	laylie
as always	he biixilie'

English	Maya
amuse	baaxal
ancient	uuchben
and	ka', yetel
angry	p'uhul
animal	aalak', ba'alche'
annatto	kiwi'
answer	nuukik
ant	sinik
anteater	chab
anus	it
approach	naats'al, naats'ik, naats'kuba
arbor	makan
area	banda
arise	liik'il
arisen	liik'a'an
armadillo	weech
arm	k'ab
armpit	xiik'
arrive	k'uchul
ask for	k'aatik
ass	u bak'el yit, bo'ox
asshole	it
at	ti'
atole	sa', saka'

English	Maya
avocado	on
awake	ahal
awaken	aahal
axe	baat

B

back	pach
bad	k'as
bag	sabukan
bake	tahal
balls	ye'el toon
banana	ha'as
bark	sool
base	chun, haal
basket	xak, xuux
bat	soots'
bathe	ichkiil
be	yan
beak	koh
bean	bu'ul
beard	me'ex
beat	hats'ik, p'uchik
beautiful	hats'uts
beauty	hats'utsil
because	tumen
bedbug	pik

English	Maya
bee	kaab
beer	cheba, seerbeesa
before	taan, yaax
beginning	chun
begin	chunbesik, chunpa-hal, kaahsik
behind	pach
belly	nak'
belong	
belonging to	ti'al
below	kaabal, yaanal
belt	k'axab nak'
bend	wats'ik, wuuts'ik
beneath	yaanal
beside	tseel
big	nohoch, nuuk, nukuch
bird	baach, ch'iich'
birth	sihil
bit	xet'
a bit	hump'iit
bite	chi'bal, paap, paapil
bitter	k'aah
black	box
blind	ch'oop
block	sup'ik

English	Maya
blond	chakxiich', ch'el
blood	k'iik'
blow	uustik
blue	ya'ax
boar	kitam
body	winklil
boil	chaakik, tahal
bone	baak
book	hu'un
born	sihil
bosom	iim
boss	nohchil
bother	p'uhsik
bower	makan
boy	paal, xi'paal
brains	ts'o'om
branch	k'ab
bread	waah, pan
break	kaachik, pa'ik, puch'ik
broken	chinga'an, kaacha'al
breakfast	uk'ul
breathe	ch'a'ik iik'
bring	taasik
bring out	ho'sik

English	Maya
broad	kooch
broom	miis
broth	k'aab, k'ool
brother	iits'in, suku'un
brush	k'aax
cut brush	paak
brushhook	xloob
bucket	ch'ooy
building	nahil
bull	wakax
bullfight	pay wakax
burden	kuch
burn	elel, paap, took, tookik
burst	waak'al, xiikik
bury	mukik
busted	chinga'an
butterfly	pepem
buttocks	bo'ox
buy	manik
buzzard	ch'oom
by	tumen

C

English	Maya
cactus	paak'am
calf (of the leg)	t'oon

English	Maya
call	pay
callous	t'aaham
can	tan u pahtal
cannot	mu pahtal
candle	kib
care for, take	kanantik, ta'akik
care of	
carry	kuchik
case	pix
cat	mis
catch	chukik
cattle	wakax
cave	aktun
celebration	cha'an
cement	u chun pak'
center	chumuk
change	k'exik, k'eexil
charcoal	chuuk
chat	tsikbal
cheap	ma' ko'ohi'
chew	hach'ik
chicken	kaax
child	paal
chin	k'ono'ch
chocolate	chokwa'
cigarette	chamal

English	Maya
citrus fruit	pak'aal
clean	hanil, miistik, sak,
	utskintik
clear (*adj.*)	hanil, saas
clear (*v.*)	paak
climb	na'akal
close	k'alik, k'aalal,
	sup'ik
clothes	nook'
clothing	nook'
cloud	mu(n)yal
cloudy	nookoy, puuk'
coatimundi	chi'ik
cob	bakal
coffee	boxha', kaape
coil	kopik, to'ik
cold	ke'el, siis, se'en
comb	t'eel, xaache',
	xaachetik
come	ko'oten, tak, tal
come out	hook'ol
completely	humpuli
constantly	sansamal
consume	
be consumed	xuupul
consumé	kaldo kaax

English	Maya
content	kimak ool
continue	segertik
convenient	ki'
cook	tahal
cooked	tak'aan
cooking-pit	piib
cool	ke'el, siis,
	siskuntik
copulate	ts'iis
corn	nal, xi'im, t'aaham
cornmeal	k'u'um, sakan
cornmeal	sa', saka'
beverage	
cotton	pits'
cough	se'en
count	xook, xookik
cover	pix
cow	wakax
coyote	ch'amak, ch'omak
crocodile	aayin
crowded	babahki
crush	puch'ik
crushed	sahkab, saskab
limestone	
cry	awat, ook'ol
curse	maldisyontik

English	Maya
custom	suuk
cut	ch'aakik, k'osik, t'ookik, xotik

D

daily	sansamal
dance	ook'ot
dangerous	hach k'as u bin
dark	e'hoch'e'en
become dark	e'hoch'e'ntal
dawn	saastal
day	k'iin
dead	kimen
deaf	kook
deaf-mute	tootkook
dear	xun
debris	sohol
deep	taam
deer	keeh, yuuk
defecate	ta'kuba
deliver	k'ubik
demon	xtaabay
descend	eemel
devil	kisiin
dick	toon
die	kimil

English	Maya
different	hela'an
difficult	yah
dig	paanik
digit	aal
diligent	aalkab u man meyah, seeb u meyah
dinner	o'och
direct	toh
dirt	lu'um
dirty	eek'
disappear	saatal
disrobe	pitik
distance	naachil
distant	naach
distinct	hela'an
disturb	p'uhsik
divide	hatsik, t'ooxik
do	beetik
doctor	ts'ats'aak
dog	pek'
done	ts'ook
dove	uukum
dragonfly	turix
dream	naay, wayak'
dress	iipil, piik

English	Maya
drink	kaltal, uk'ul, uk'ik
drum	tunk'ul
drunk	kala'an
get drunk	kaltal
dry	hayk'intik, tihil, tihsik
dried	hayk'inta'an, tikin
dumb	toot, ts'u'uy pol
dung	ta'
dusk	bin ka aak'abtal
dye	bon

E

English	Maya
ear	xikin
early	hatskab k'in
earlier	behla'ak, ka'chi, yaax
earth	kab, lu'um
east	lak'in
eat	hanal, hantik
edge	haal
egg	he'
either	**wa**
elbow	kuuk
embarrassment	su'tal
embrace	meek'ik

English	Maya
end	ts'ook, hool, xul
enough	hach ya'ab
enter	oko(l)
entrance	hool
epiphyte	ch'u
errand	tusbel
error	si'pil
escape	luk'ul, puuts'ul
evening	okaank'iin
evil	k'as, loobil
exchange	k'eexel
excrement	ta'
expect	pa'tik
expensive	ko'oh
explain	tsoolik
explode	wak'al, xiikik
extend	sats'ik
extinguish	tuupik
extract	ho'sik
extremely	sen
eye	ich

F

face	ich
faded	poos
fair (complexion)	chakxiich', ch'eel

English	Maya
falcon	koos
fall	lubul
false(hood)	tuus
family	lak'tsil
fang	ts'a'ay
far	naach
farm	kol
fart	kis, kiskuba
fast	seeb, seeban
fat (*adj.*)	polok
fat (*n.*)	tsaats
father	tat(a), papah
fault	kuch, si'pil
fear	sahkil
feather	k'uk'um
feed	tseentik
feel	u'yik
ferret	saabin
fertile	
fertile soil	siis lu'um
field	kol
fifty-fifty	chunchumuk
fight	ba'te'el
fill	chup(s)ik, chuupul
find	kaaxtik
find out	oheltik

English	Maya
finger	aal
fingernail	iich'ak
finish	ts'oksik
fire	k'aak'
firearm	ts'oon
firewood	si'
firm	hets'a'an
first	yaaxil
fish	kay
fist	wool a k'ab
fixed	heets'a'an
flat	hay, peka'an, taax
flatten	pak'achtik
flatten tortillas	pak'ach
flatulate	kiskuba
flatulence	kis
flee	luk'ul
flint	tok'tunich
flour	sakan
flower	lol, nikte'
flute	piitoo
foam	yoon
fold	wuuts'ik
follow	tsaypachtik
foot	ook
for	ti'al

English	Maya
force	muuk'
foreigner	ts'ul, xunaan
forest	k'aax
forget	tu'ub, tu'ubsik,
	tu'ubul
fountain	sayab
four	kan-
fox	ch'amak, ch'omak
fresh	aak', tumben, siis
	ool
fried	tsahbil
friend	amigoo
frighten	sahbesik
frog	muuch
front	taan, taanil
fruit	ch'uhuk, yich
fry	tsahik
fuck	ts'iis, topik
full	chuup

G

gather	t'okik
gay	ch'uupul xib
gentleman	yuum
ghost	xtaabay
gift	siibil

English	Maya
girl	ch'uupal
give	ts'ik, siik
gnat	us
gnome	k'at
go	bin, ko'ox, xi'ik, ximbal
go out	hook'ol
goat	taman
gold	taak'in
good	ma'aloob, uts
good-looking	ki'ichpam
good luck!	xi'ik tech utsil
gourd	chuuh, homa', luch
grab	machik
grandfather	tat(a)
grandmother	chiich, mamich
grasp	ch'a'ik, maachik
grass	su'uk
green	ya'ax
griddle	xamach
grill	k'a'atik
grilled	k'a'bil, pok chuuk
ground (earth)	lu'um
ground (grind)	huch'bil, muxbil
grow	ch'iihil
grown	ch'iiha'an, nuuktak

English	Maya
gruel	k'eyem
guava	pichi'
gun	ts'oon

H

hail	bat
hair	tso'ts
half	chumuk
hammock	k'aan
hand	k'ab
hang	ch'uuyul,
	ch'uykintik,
	sinik
happen	uuchul
happy	kiimak ool
hard	yah
harsh	k'a'am
harvest	hooch, hoochik
hat	p'ook
hatchet	baat
hate	p'ektik
hateful	p'eka'an
have	yan
have someone	xi'ik ———
———	
hay	su'uk

English	Maya
head	ho'ol, pol
headache	k'inam ho'ol/pol
heal	ts'aakik
hear	u'yik
heart	puksik'al
hearth	k'ooben
heat	chokokintik,
	chokwil
heavy	aal
heel	tuunkuy
help	aantik
helper	aantah
hemp	kih
hen	xkaax
herb	xiw
herbalist	hmen
here	te', te'la', waye'
here it is	he'la'
hide (skin)	k'ewel
hill	muul
hoarse	ma' kal
hole	hool
home	nahil, otoch
honey	kaab
hop	siit'
horn	baak

English	Maya
horse	tsimin
hot	chokow, k'ilkab, k'iinal, paap
house	nah
how	biix
how many	haytul, hayp'el
how much	baahux
humid	k'ilkab
hummingbird	ts'unu'un
hungry	wi'ih
hunter	ts'oonol, ts'oonero
hurricane	chich iik'
hurry	seeb, seebak
hurt	kinbesik, kinpahal, yah
husband	iicham
husk	sool

I

English	Maya
I	ten
if	wa
ignite	t'aabik
iguana	huh
ill	k'oha'an
illness	k'oha'nil
become ill	k'oha'ntal

English	Maya
imagine	ts'iboltik
immediately	beoritasa, napulak
important	k'ana'an
improve	utskintik
in	ti'
incapacitated	nuum
incite	pay
incline	niix
Indian	masewal, maya
injury	loob
insert	oksik
inside	ich(il)
intestines	chooch
introduce	oksik
iron	maskab
itch	sak'

J

jaguar	chakmool
jay	ch'el
jicama	chiikam
joke	baaxal
juice	k'aab
jump	siit'
jungle	k'aax
just	sam

English	Maya
K	
kill	kinsik
kiss	ts'u'uts', ts'u'uts'ik
kitchen	k'ooben
knee	piix
knife blade	u yeh kuchiyo
know	kanik, k'ahol,
	k'ahot(ik), ohel

English	Maya
L	
lacking	xma'
land	lu'um
landmark	xu'uk'
language	t'aan
large	nohoch, nukuch
lasso	suum
late	ka'ka't, xaanal
later	ka'ka't(e')
laugh	che'eh
lazy	hoykep
leaf	le'
league	luub
learn	kanik
leather	k'ewel
leathery	ts'u'uy

English	Maya
leave	hatsik, hook'ol, luk'ul, p'atik
left	ts'iik
leg	ook
lend	mahantik
length	chowakil
let	ko'ox, xi'ik, yanak
letter	hu'un
level	hay, taax
lie	tus, tusik
lie down	chi(l)tal
light (n.)	saasil
become light	saastal
light (v.)	t'aabik
light (weight)	saal
lightning	u hats' chaak
like	
I like it	uts tin wich
lima bean	iib
lime (calcium carbonate)	ta'an
little	chan, chichan, mehen, ma' ya'abi'
a little	hump'iit
little by little	huhump'iitil
live	kuxtal

English	Maya
liver	taaman
living	kuxa'an
lizard	huh, meerech, toolok
load	kuch
loan	mahantik
locust	saak'
long	chowak
look	paktik
look for	kaaxtik
lord	yuum, yuntsil
lose	saatik
get lost	saatal
lost	saata'an
louse	uk'
love	yakuntik
low	taam
lower	ensik

M

machete	maskab, xtaats'
maiden	suhuy paal
make	mak'antik, meetik
make-believe	tuus
male	xib
man	maak, winik, xib

English	Maya
many	ya'abkach, ya'abo'ob, ya'ab
marijuana	k'uuts
marry	ts'okol beel
masonry	pak'
matter	beel
may	hu' chabale'
may not	mu chabal
maybe	beyts'abile', wal(e')
me	ten
meal	hanal, hanlil, o'och
measure	p'isik
meat	bak'
mecate	p'isik'aan
medicine	ts'aak
metate and mano	k'abka'
middle	chumuk
midnight	chumuk aak'ab
milling place	k'uch huch'bil
milpa	kol
mind	ool
mirror	neen
misfortune	loob
mist	ye'eb
mix	xaak'tik

English	Maya
moist	ch'uul
moisten	ch'uulik
become moist	ch'uultul
money	taak'in
monkey	tuucha
moon	luunaa
morning	hatskab k'iin
mosquito	k'oxol
mouth	chi'
move	peeksik
much	ya'ab
not much	ma' ya'abi'
mucus	siim
muddy	puuk'
muggy	k'as k'ilkab
music	k'aay, paax

N

naked	xma' nook'
name	k'aaba'
narrow	koom
native	wayile'
near	naats'
necessary	k'abeet, k'ana'an
necessity	nu'kul

English	Maya
neck	kal
needle	puuts'
nest	k'u'
nettles	laal
never	mixbik'in
new	tumben
nice	ki', hats'uts
night	aak'ab
nightmare	k'as wayak'
no	ma', ma'tan,
	ma'tech
no one	mixmaak
noise	ch'e'eh
make noise	huum
noon	chumuk k'iin
north	xaman
nose	ni'
not	ma', ma'tan
nothing	mixba'al
now	beora
nowhere	mixtu'ux

O

o.k.	ma'aloob
obligation	kuch

English	Maya
obtain	k'amik
odor	book, ch'e'eh
old	biyeho, nohoch, nuxib, uuchben
old woman	xnuk
omen	tamax chi'
on	chika'an, ti'
one	hump'el, huntul, hunts'it
open	heebik, heebel, heeba'an
opening	chi', hool
opossum	ooch
or	wa
orange	china, pak'aal
order	tusbeltik
put in order	tsool
origin	chun
oriole	k'ubul
other	heel, laak'
overcast	nookoy
become overcast	nokoytal
overtake	chukpachtik
owl	tunkuruchu
owner	yuumil

English	Maya
P	
paca	haaleb
pack	but'ik
pain	k'iinam, yah
paint	bon, bonik
pale	poos
palpitate	peek
pants	eex
papaya	put
paper	hu'un
parrot	t'uut'
pass	mansik
pass by	maan
pay	bo'otik
peccary	kitam
penetrate	pot
penis	toon
pensive	tuukul
pepper	ik
perceive	u'yik
perfect	hach beyo'
perhaps	kensa biixi', talbes, wal(e')
permit	chaik
person	maak, winik
pet	aalak'

English	Maya
physician	ts'ats'aak
piece	xet'
pig	k'eek'en
pillar	okom
pillow	k'aanho'ol
piss	wiix
pit	
cooking pit	piib
place	banda, kaah, kahtal, tu'ux
plant	pak'al
play	baaxal, baaxtik
plum	abal
pointed	yeh
polish	yuultik
poor	otsil
porcupine	k'i'xooch
portion	xet'
possible	beyts'abile'
if possible	he u beeta'ale'
it is possible	hu' beeta'ale'
it is not possible	mixtaan u beeta'al
post	okom
pound	pak'achtik
pregnant	k'oha'an, yo'om
prepare	mak'antik

English	Maya
previously	ka'chi, uuchilak
price	tohol
problem	ba'te'el
prognostication	tamax chi'
pull	koolik, paaytik
puma	koh
pumpkin	k'uum
pumpkin seed	sikil
punch	looxik
pursue	chukpachtik
pus	puh
put	ts'ik, oksik
put on (clothes)	bukintik
put out (fire, light)	tuupik
pyramid	muul

Q

quail	beech'
queer	ch'upul xib
quick	seeb, seebak
quickly	seeba'an

R

rabbit	t'u'ul
raccoon	k'ulu'
rain	chaak, ha', k'aaxal

English	Maya
raise	li'sik
rat	ch'o'
read	xook, xookik
ready	saame, ts'ook
get ready	li'skuba
receive	k'amik
recognize	k'ahot(ik)
red	chak
reed	siit
relative	ch'iilankabil, laak',
	lak'tsil, pamilya
remain	p'atal
remember	k'ahot(ik)
repair	utskintik
reprimand	k'eeyik
resin	its
rest	he'lel
rest oneself	he'skuba
return	suut, sutik
rich	ayik'al, taak'inal
right	no'oh
to the right	no'ha'an
right away	beorita, napulak
ripe	k'an, tak'aan, yi'h
ripen	yi'htal
rise	liik'il

English	Maya
road	beh, beel
roast	k'a'atik
roasted	k'a'bil, pokbil
rock	tuunich
roof	u ho'ol nah, u pol nah
rooster	t'eel
root	mots
rope	suum
rose	lol
round	woolis
rub	yuultik
ruin	loobil
run	aalkab, chika'an
rust	its

S

sack	sabukan
sad	tuukul
salesman	konol
saleswoman	xkonol
salt	ta'ab, ta'bsik
same	laylie
sapodilla	ya'
say	a'alik, t'aan
saying	t'aan

English	Maya
scare	sahbesik
scold	k'eeyik
scorpion	sina'an
scram!	huchi, xen te'lo'
scrape	paanik
see	ilik
seed	i'nah, neek'
seek, look for	kaaxtik
sell	konik
send	tuuxtik
sew	chuuy
shade, shadow	bo'oy
shake	peeksik, tiital, tiitik
shaman	hmen
shame	su'tal
share	t'ooxik
sharp	yeh
sharpness	paapil
shave	ts'ikik
shaven	ts'ika'an
shawl	booch'
sheep	taman
shell	sool
shit	ta', ta'kuba
shoe	xanab

English	Maya
shoot	ts'oonik
short	koom
shoulder	kelembaal
show	e'esik, tsikbatik
shuck (corn)	oxo'ontik
sick	k'oha'an
side	haal, tseel
sin	k'eban, si'pil, loobil
sing	k'aay
single	hun
sinkhole	ts'onot
sister	kiik, iits'in
sit	kulal
size	nohochil
what size?	buka'ah?
skin	k'ewel
skinny	ts'oya'an
skull	ho'ol
skunk	payooch
sky	ka'an
slab	hayam
sleep	wenel
slender	bek'ech
slimy	hahalki, hoholki
slingshot	tiraule
slippery	hahalki, hoholki

English	Maya
slope	niix
slow	chaambeel
small	chan, chichan, mehen
smallest part	t'uup
smell	bok, u'yik bok
smoke	buts', ts'uuts', ts'uuts'ik
snail	urich
snake	kan
snare	peets'
snot	siim
soil	lu'um
someone	wa maax
something	wa ba'ax
somewhat	k'as
somewhere	wa tu'ux
son	paal
song	k'aay
soot	sabak
soul	pixan
sour	pah
soursop	oop
south	nohol
sow	pak'al, pak'ik
sown	pak'a'an

English	Maya
spark	xikin k'aak'
speak	t'aanik
spicy	paap
spider	am
spill	weekik
spilled	weeka'an
spine	t'o'ol a pach
spirit	iik', pixan
spouse	laak', pamilyah
spring	sayab, sayap ha'
spy	ch'uktik
squash	k'uum
squeak	kirits'
squirrel	ku'uk
stand	wa'tal
stand on one's feet	wa'akuba
star	ek'
start	ketik
stay	p'atal
steal	ookol, ooklik
steep	niix
stem	chun
step-(relation)	mahan
stew	k'ool
stick	che', xuul

English	Maya
stick around	xaantal
stiff	t'iinil
stocked	babahki
stomach	nak'
stone	tuunich, sahkab, saskab
stool	k'aanche'
stop	wa'tal
stopped	wa'bal
storm	chich iik'
straight	toh
stranger	ts'ul, xunaan
strap	k'axab nak'
straw	siit
stretch	sats'ik
strike	p'uchik
strong	chich, k'a'am
stuff	but'ik
submerge	t'ubik
suck	ts'u'uts', ts'u'uts'ik
sugar	ch'uhuk
sun	k'iin
sunset	bin ka aak'abtal
sunken	t'uba'an
super	sen uts, sen ma'aloob

English	Maya
sweet	ch'uhuk
sweet potato	is
swim	baab
swollen	chuup

T

tail	neh
take	ch'a'ik, bisik
take care (of)	kanantik
take off	tokik
tamale	tamali'
tame	suk
tangled	so'sook
tarantula	chi(n)wol
tasty	ki'
tayra	saamho'ol, saampol
teach	ka'nsik
teacher	ka'nsah
teat	iim
tell	tsikbatik
tense	t'iinil
testicles	ye'el toon
thank you	dyos bo'otik
that	ka', lelo'
thatch palm	xa'an
then	tuun

English	Maya
there	te', te'lo'
there is/are	yan
there isn't/aren't	(mi)na'an
therefore	la'tene
thick	piim, polok
thickness	polkil
thin	bek'ech, hay
thing	ba'al
think	tuukul, tuklik
thirsty	uk'ah
this (one)	lela'
thorn	k'i'ix
three	oxp'el, oxtul
throat	kal
throb	peek
throw	ch'iin
thrush	pich'
thunder	huum chaak
tick (insect)	pech
tie	k'aaxik
tilt	nixik
time	k'iin
tin can	laataa
tire	ka'nah
tired	ka'na'an, ch'a'ik ool
to	ti'

English	Maya
toad	muuch
toasted	oop', pokbil
tobacco	k'uuts
today	behla'(e'), behla'ak
together	et, mul
tomato	p'aak
tomorrow	saamal
day after tomorrow	ka'beh
tongue	ak'
tool	nu'kul
tooth	koh
toothpick	ch'ilib
tortilla	waah
totally	humpuli
toucan	piitoreal
tough	chich, ts'u'uy
toward	tak
town	kaah
trap	peets', pets'tik
trash	sohol
tree	che'
trick	kechtik
true	haah
truth	haahil

English	Maya
trunk	chun
turkey	kuts, tso', uulum
turtle	aak
twig	ch'ilib
twins	k'uho'b
two	ka'p'el, ka'tul

U

English	Maya
understand	na'atik
untidy	loob
untie	wach'ik
until	tak
up	ka'anal
uproot	t'ookik
upset	
don't get upset	ma hak'al a wool
urinate	wiix
urine	wiix
us	to'on
use	baaxtik, ch'a'ik
useless	nuum
used	
be used up	xuupul
I'm used to it	suuk ten
utensil	nu'kul

English	Maya
V	
vendor	konol
very	hach
vine	ak'
virgin	suhuy
visit	ximbatik
voice	kal
vomit	xeh
W	
wait	pa'tal, pa'tik
walk	ximbal
wall	pak'
want	k'aat, taak
warm	chokow
wart	aax
wash	p'o'ik
wasp	xux
water	ha'
wave	payk'ab
way	
that way	beyo'
this way	beya'
waylay	ch'uktik
we	to'on

English	Maya
weasel	saabin
weave	wak'
wedding	ts'okol beel
weed	k'aax, su'uk
weep	ook'ol
weigh	p'isik
well (*adv.*)	ma'aloob, uts
well (*n.*)	ch'e'en, sayap ha'
west	chik'in
wet	ch'uul
what	ba'ax
what about	kuux
when	ba'ax k'iin, ba'ax
	ora, bik'ix, ka'
where	tu'ux
which	makalmak
whip	hats'ik
whistle	piitoo, xuxub
white	sak
white man	ts'ul
white woman	xunaan
who	maax
whoever	he' maaxe'
why	ba'axten, ba'en
wide	kooch

English	Maya
wife	atan
wild	k'o'ox
wild animal	ba'alche'
winch	pechech
wind	iik'
wing	xiik'
witch	xwaay
with	yetel
without	xma'
wizard	waay
woman	ko'olel, xch'up,
	xunaan, xnuk
wood	che'
work	meyah
world	kab
worm	lukum, nok'ol
worthless	mu baler mixba'al,
	mixtun baler
wound	loob
write	ts'iib, ts'ii(b)tik
wrong	k'eban

Y

yam	is
year	ha'ab

English	Maya
yellow	k'an
yes	he'le'
yesterday	ho'lyak
you	tech, te'ex
youth	xi'paal

Index